CHARACTERS OF
THE REFORMATION

CHARACTERS OF THE REFORMATION

By
HILAIRE BELLOC

CAVALIER BOOKS
MILWAUKEE, WISCONSIN

Copyright © Hilaire Belloc 1936.
First published by Sheed and Ward, London 1936.
Retypeset and republished by Cavalier Books, Milwaukee 2015.
Cover: *Portrait of Henry VIII* by the studio of Hans Holbein the Younger c. 1537.

ISBN: 0991560698
ISBN-13: 978-0-9915606-9-1

Cavalier Books

CONTENTS

NATURE OF THE REFORMATION 7

KING HENRY VIII 20

CATHERINE OF ARAGON 30

ANNE BOLEYN 40

THOMAS CROMWELL 48

SAINT THOMAS MORE 55

POPE CLEMENT THE SEVENTH 62

THOMAS CRANMER 68

STEPHEN GARDINER 76

MARY TUDOR 83

QUEEN ELIZABETH 90

MARY STUART 96

WILLIAM CECIL 104

HENRY IV OF FRANCE 110

JAMES I OF ENGLAND 117

FERDINAND II 123

GUSTAVUS ADOLPHUS 131

RICHELIEU 137

LAUD 142

OLIVER CROMWELL 148

RENE DESCARTES 155

BLAISE PASCAL 160

WILLIAM OF ORANGE 165

LOUIS XIV 173

NATURE OF THE REFORMATION

THE break-up of united western Christendom with the coming of the Reformation was by far the most important thing in history since the foundation of the Catholic Church fifteen hundred years before.

Men of foresight perceived at the time that if catastrophe were allowed to consummate itself, if the revolt were to be successful (and it was successful) our civilization would certainly be imperilled and possibly, in the long run, destroyed.

That indeed is what has happened. Europe with all its culture is now seriously imperilled and stands no small chance of being destroyed by its own internal disruption; and all this is ultimately the fruit of the great religious revolution which began four hundred years ago.

That being so, the Reformation being of this importance, it ought to form the chief object of historical study in modern times, and its nature should be clearly understood even if only in outline.

Now to understand the Reformation it is not enough to appreciate how it arose and what sort of men conducted the battle on either side when the struggle had broken out. It is equally important and, perhaps, more important to appreciate that the affair went, like all great conflicts in history, through certain phases which perpetually recur in human disputes.

All great conflicts begin with an uncertain phase during which one does not know which side will prevail, or whether either will prevail. After that phase comes a second phase which may be one of two things: it may be the increasingly apparent victory of one side over the other, or it may be stalemate—a drawn battle.

Even if one of the two conflicting original opponents, either those who are for change or those who are for tradition, secures a victory, the result is affected by the struggle. No victory, however complete on the part of the conservatives, can make things return to exactly the same state as they were in before the challenge was thrown down. No victory, however complete on the part of the revolutionaries, can ever wholly get rid of the past, which will always remain intertwined with the fibre of the men who were moulded by it.

But still, a complete victory on one side or the other does usually produce an enduring state of things. When there is a stalemate, that is, a drawn battle, the result is otherwise. In that case there continues a further series of changes due to the survival in power of either combatant.

The two camps remain in activity—the one opposed to the other, reacting one against the other—and there will be consequently a chain of developments which continuously produces new effects as the generations proceed.

As an example of the first sort of thing—a complete victory—we have the success of our civilization against the Albigenses. That sect at one moment bid fair to break up Europe, but the orthodox armies, the orthodox monarchs and leaders and the Papacy won. The result was the secure state of affairs which made the western world safe for Catholicism for centuries. An example of the opposite—of the drawn battle or stalemate—was the great Mahommedan effort beginning in the seventh century. It failed to overwhelm Christendom, but it had a sufficient success to establish a great new culture over against Europe and hostile to Europe, with the result that for centuries the two opponents remained intact, and perpetually reacted one upon the other.

In the case of the Reformation it looked at one moment as though the side of authority and tradition was going to have a complete victory; in which case we should have today a settled and secure Europe, united again in the Catholic Faith.

Unfortunately that victory was never won, and the upshot of the struggle, after a hundred and thirty years, was the division of European civilization into two halves, the Protestant culture and the Catholic culture. As for the third—the eastern part—the culture attaching to the Greek Church, it did not much affect modern times between the outbreak of the Reformation and the rise of Russia two hundred years ago.

The universal, spiritual and therefore social upheaval, generally called "The Reformation," lasted from its inception to its conclusion as an open struggle, about two hundred years.

You may take 1688, the exile of *James II* (or 1715, the failure of the Jacobite effort at a moment when there was still a living Catholic body in England), as the end of a conflict which clearly opens in the German revolt of 1517.

It ran through these stages:—

During the first twenty years or so, from 1517 onwards, the revolt against the Church was closely intermixed with a very legitimate determination to reform abuses. It was not easy to see on which side a man or a book or an argument lay. There were grave corruptions in the Church and grave discontent with the organization of the Church on the part of masses of men who never dreamed of destroying Church unity or interfering with the great mass of Church doctrine and custom. This was especially the case in England, where the Church was less corrupt than elsewhere and where the people were by nature conservative.

But at the end of these twenty years there came—round about 1536–40—a change in what had hitherto been a confused movement.

This change was primarily caused by the great effect of Calvin, who set out with the greatest lucidity and unparalleled energy to form a counter-Church for the destruction of the old Church. He it was who really made the *new* religion, wholly hostile to the old one. At the same time the temptation to loot Church property and the habit of doing so had appeared and was growing; and this rapidly created a vested interest in promoting the change in religion. Those who attacked Catholic doctrine, as, for instance, in the matters of the celibacy in the monastic Orders, or of a divinely appointed Hierarchy with the Papacy at its summit, opened the door for the seizure of the enormous clerical endowments, monastic, episcopal and parochial, by the Princes and City Corporations. Men already individually powerful through their wealth, especially through their ownership of land, joined in the rapine. The property of convents and monasteries passed wholesale to the looters over great areas of Christendom: Scandinavia, the British Isles, the Northern Netherlands, much of the Germanies and many of the Swiss Cantons. The endowments of hospitals, colleges, schools, guilds, were largely though not wholly seized. Those of the clergy and hierarchy, the lands supporting Bishoprics and Chapters and parish clergy, were robbed of from seven-eighths to half of their value.

Such an economic change in so short a time our civilization had never seen.

It had for effect the firm establishment of a permanent motive for confirming the success of the Religious Revolution. The new adventurers and the older gentry who had so suddenly enriched themselves, saw, in the return of Catholicism, peril to their immense new fortunes.

It is about this time, therefore, a generation after the first revolt, that there arises a distinct effort to impose in various places new laws and institutions to the destruction of Catholicism.

After the middle of the sixteenth century (from 1550–60) that change is clearly apparent, and, with it, fighting begins: fighting on the part of Catholic Europe to suppress the new Protestant Governments, fighting on the part of these Governments to suppress Catholicism in their own provinces; and in places civil war between the two parties. That fighting goes on during all the second half of the century, roughly from 1550–60 to, say, 1605–1610. There was fighting in Scotland, the beginning of what was to be an unending attempt to destroy Catholicism in Ireland by force; fighting in the Netherlands; but the most critical and violent of all the fighting was in France. On the issue of the religious wars in France depended the preservation or destruction of Catholicism in Europe.

Oddly enough, the German Empire, which was nominally ruled from Vienna, was spared, and enjoyed peace compared with these other places. It was there that the Reformation had broken out, and yet successive Emperors—by compromise, also from lack of power because so many of their subordinate Princes and Cities were practically independent—managed to keep the peace.

But meanwhile the Catholic forces in Europe had tardily woken up, and there had been started what is generally called the "Counter Reformation."

But neither the Counter Reformation nor the active fighting which succeeded in preserving a part of Christendom intact, would have been necessary *but for difficult success of the Protestant movement in England.*

This is the most important point to seize in all the story of the great religious revolution, and it is the point least often insisted on.

The early enthusiasm for change was anarchic and dispersed. It had no form. It was of a violence which was bound to burn itself out, especially as it was resisted by all the organized *central* authorities of Christendom: the Kings and the Emperor. All that descended directly from the ancient foundation of our culture, the Romanized, civilized core of Europe, held out—save for one province: Britain.

England was captured for the Revolutionary side, not by any desire on the part of her people, but by a succession of incidents which marked each of them a step more difficult to retrace.

First, on a matter in no way connected with the Faith, the King of England, the most complete autocrat of his day, happened to quarrel with the Pope. The divorce of *Henry VIII* from his wife *Catherine of Aragon*, due to his infatuation with Anne Boleyn, began the business. It was conducted by a man of far greater ability than *Henry*, one *Thomas Cromwell*, an adventurer of high talent and no scruples (the great-uncle of Oliver and founder of the vast Cromwell fortune of which Oliver was a cadet). This Thomas Cromwell advised and carried out the confiscation of the monastic lands in England; a huge loot which was to be followed by further robbery of clerical endowments of every kind, including schools and colleges as well as the wealth of Sees and Parishes and Chapters. The new fortunes arising from this flood of confiscation determined the issue.

At the outset of the last quarrel with the Papacy some few Englishmen had stood out for the Supremacy of the Pope and the consequent unity of Christendom. The most prominent of them and the best venerated is *St. Thomas More*. Henry, the king, had for ecclesiastical agent in his divorce one *Thomas Cranmer* whom he made Archbishop of Canterbury and who proclaimed the schism with Rome: an ardent opponent of the whole Catholic scheme at heart, and particularly of the Mass and Blessed Sacrament—though as long as Henry lived he dared not show his true feelings too openly, for Henry was, to the last, firm and even devout in his adherence to Catholic doctrine and especially to the Holy Sacrifice of the Mass and the Real Presence in the Blessed Sacrament.

A contrast to Cranmer, and typical of the official England of this time, which led a people confused and bewildered by the new papal quarrel, was *Stephen Gardiner*, Henry's Bishop of Winchester. When it was too late and after Henry was dead he was appalled to see where Henry's personal quarrel with the Pope (which he had heartily supported) had led; he strongly affirmed his full Catholicism and attempted to save that of the country.

At Henry's death a rickety child, his diseased little son Edward, nominally succeeded. But real power was, of course, in the hands of the unscrupulous men who formed the Council. They rigorously pursued and increased the loot of religious endowments and even made an effort to impose a new Protestant religion repugnant to the vast majority of Englishmen (the secretary to the Government, who had all the evidence available, sets that majority at eleven-twelfths of the people).

Edward died and, by Henry's will, his half-sister, Catherine of Aragon's daughter, *Mary Tudor*, succeeded.

Mary Tudor was received with wild popular rejoicing as the restorer of the old national religion of Englishmen and the legitimate queen, and the end—it was hoped—of oppressive government by a clique of upstart rich men. To save the country from Franco-Scottish domination she married Philip, the heir to Spain. The marriage was not popular and the English Council, against the advice of Philip and to show their independence of him, began a violent persecution of the still small Protestant minority. This persecution of the small but intense revolutionary group was especially violent in London and, though not unpopular—yet did not receive any popular support. Neutral men, as always, attested in favour of the sufferers.

Therefore when Mary died after a brief reign of half a dozen years, her half-sister, *Elizabeth*, succeeded her. Elizabeth was accepted with the greater ease in that she had professed Catholicism loudly and had taken the oath to preserve it. But she would not have got the throne but for the support of her brother-in-law, Philip of Spain, who hoped to marry her as he had married Mary, and who regarded her as a counterweight to France, his chief rival.

During Elizabeth's long reign she stood contrasted with and opposed to *Mary Stuart*, Queen of Scotland who stood for the old religion, and against whom, after a brief reign, her chief subjects rebelled. She took refuge in England where she was kept imprisoned by the English Government till they put her to death many years after.

But the true author of the great change which comes with Elizabeth and gains strength as her long reign proceeds, was a man of exceptional genius, *William Cecil*. He it was who, with Philip of Spain, put Elizabeth on the throne and ruled in her name. He saw that his new wealth was in danger so long as Catholicism remained strong in England, and proceeded to stamp it out. He it was who effected that gradual and profound change in English affairs by which the country was lost to the Faith.

That severance of England from Europe and from Christendom was, I have said, the pivotal matter of the Protestant advance. On it the partial success of the religious revolution everywhere depended. Hence the necessity for beginning by an understanding of the *English* tragedy, failing which the disruption of Europe and all our modern chaos would never have appeared.

It was coincidentally with the beginning of the turn over in England, with the second half of the sixteenth century, that there began that effort against shipwreck which, I have said, is generally called "The Counter Reformation."

Vigorous Popes undertook, unfortunately too late, the reform of abuses; the Franciscans took on a new missionary activity for the recovery of districts lost to the Faith; a General Council (which the Popes before the Reformation had especially avoided because only a little while before General Councils had proved so dangerous to unity), was summoned and is known to history as "The Council of Trent." The most important single factor in the whole of this reaction was the militant and highly disciplined body proceeding from the genius of St. Ignatius Loyola. It came to be known by the name which was first a nick-name, but later generally adopted, of "the Jesuits." These, by their discipline, singleness of aim and heroism, were the spearhead of the counter-attack. They were very nearly successful in England, they had very great effect in South Germany, and later in Poland. All these forces, combined, made for a general restoration of Catholicism.

There followed during the seventeenth century, from about 1600–1615 to 1690–1700, a ding-dong struggle between the now rooted new religion in the areas where governments had gone Protestant and the remaining Catholic bulk of Europe.

The effort to recover England had failed; Scandinavia had been turned over just as England had under the impulse of those who saw their opportunity for looting Church lands and their determination to keep this booty after the new wealth had been seized; and the northern part of the Netherlands (which have since come to be known as Holland) still maintained itself with difficulty against its lawful Sovereign, the King of Spain. But, in Europe as a whole, the tide was setting for a restoration of Catholicism, which might have been universal. In England such a restoration was rendered more difficult by the character of *James I's* reign (1603–25); in France it was rendered more possible by the character of the contemporary French King (*Henry IV*) who was assassinated in 1610. It is with these two that the story of the drawn battle in the seventeenth century opens. It is Henry IV of France yielding to the pressure of Paris, that saved Catholicism in that country. James I of England, guided and "run" by the second Cecil, William Cecil's son, Salisbury, was the man under whom, at the critical moment, England was prevented from becoming Catholic again.

Next, the *Emperor Ferdinand* in Germany set out on a kind of crusade for establishing his own authority, which had dwindled so much in the past; and at the same time for spreading Catholicism again in the parts of Germany where it had been lost. Though Catholicism in France had been saved yet the French had always lived in dread of the power of the Germans of the Empire to the east of them. Therefore, when it looked as though the Emperor Ferdinand was going to become the very powerful monarch of a united Germany, France, although as Catholic as he, determined to support his Protestant rebels against him. The French Minister who took up this policy and, therefore, is responsible before history for the failure of the Counter Reformation is the great *Richelieu*.

He found ready to his hand a singular instrument. The sparsely populated Protestant districts of Scandinavia had produced a soldier of genius, the

King of Sweden, *Gustavus Adolphus*. Richelieu put the financial resources of France at work to hire Gustavus Adolphus as an instrument for weakening the Empire and the Catholic reaction led by the Emperor Ferdinand. Gustavus Adolphus changed the art of war by his immense talent; during one dazzling year of triumph he very nearly established a Protestant German Empire more than two centuries before Bismarck: but at the height of his success he was killed in battle (1632). His effect, however, had been sufficient to prevent the Emperor from ever achieving a complete victory and from ever reuniting the Germans into one Catholic body.

Meanwhile the power of Spain was declining, and the Dutch, in what was later to be Holland, succeeded in getting their independence recognized by the King of Spain, their original sovereign.

In England the new Protestant character of the country was divided: you had one tendency expressed in *Laud*, the other expressed in the character of *Oliver Cromwell*. Oliver Cromwell and his colleagues, representing the more intense Calvinist spirit, won a Civil War which put an end to the old popular English monarchy, and during which the victors put Laud, the Archbishop of Canterbury, to death. But the main significance of Cromwell is this. That in spite of the overwhelming superiority he enjoyed in equipment and trained men he failed to destroy Catholic Ireland. He did his best. He not only massacred but—what was far more effective—he seized the land of the Irish and ruined Catholicism economically, where it had been strongest in these Islands. Yet he failed, and his failure was to prove of vast import to the fortunes of the Faith, especially in the nineteenth century.

By the middle of the seventeenth century the struggle between Catholicism and the now enthusiastic spirit which had challenged Catholicism had definitely accepted a drawn battle. The Treaties of Westphalia in 1648 established the principle that subjects should follow the religion of their Government, and within the next ten years all Europe settled down into two camps—the Catholic culture on the one side and the Protestant culture on the other.

The Catholic culture was, therefore, partially saved; but it had failed to recover Europe as a whole, and within the Church arose new movements which the Reformation had started.

At the origin of one of these was the great name of *Descartes*, at the origin of the other the great name of *Pascal*. Descartes was a man of the first half of the seventeenth century; Pascal belonged to a generation immediately younger. Descartes was almost exactly the contemporary of Cromwell, but, of course, a far greater man with an infinitely greater effect upon civilization.

Descartes introduced that idea which has dominated European thought ever since and has had such powerful effects upon the Catholic Church itself, which may be called in the best sense of the word "Rationalism."

The new expansion of physical science had begun with the sixteenth century and had been proceeding rapidly; it had been especially noticeable in the domain of astronomy, and astronomy is just that science in which we see the great laws of nature working, as it were, inexorably, and on the largest scale. Moreover, astronomy is dominated by mathematics.

Descartes set himself out to examine the whole nature of things—that is, to make a complete philosophy. The Catholic Church is itself a complete philosophy on all that concerns the chief interest of man; but the Catholic Church does not set up to provide a philosophical system, still less a philosophical system which shall be necessarily true in its explanation of the material universe.

Scholasticism, as it is called, or Thomism (from the final great work of St. Thomas Aquinas), might be called "the official philosophy" of the Church as it had stood throughout the later Middle Ages: but it was (and is) important to distinguish between this "official" acceptation of Thomism and the invariable teaching authority of the Faith. For instance, in St. Thomas' philosophy and that of his predecessors the Real Presence is expressed in the term "Trans-substantiation"; but no Catholic is bound to accept the scholastic doctrine of substance, and so long as the truth of the Real Presence is maintained (i.e. that the whole of the Humanity and Divinity of Our Lord is present in the Blessed Sacrament after the words of consecration and in either element; and that the original Bread and Wine wholly cease to be) Catholic doctrine is satisfied.

Now, Thomism had naturally declined with the decline of the Middle Ages. Scholastic disputation had degraded into what were often puerilities and debates nearly always tedious and half the time futile. It was indeed disgust with the dryness and lack of vitality of the school teaching which had largely accounted for a revolt among the younger scholars. Descartes, a whole lifetime after the beginning of the Reformation, set out to begin, if he could, the whole thing over again—to ask and settle all those questions which scholastic philosophy had also examined from the very roots. He even started with the discussion as to whether man himself, the mind originating the discussion, existed or no. He took as his starting point the undoubted truth that since a man thinks, he *is*; and on that he would base his system. In the expansion of that system he insists upon only accepting knowledge that is "proved," and that is where he had so great an influence upon all the thought which followed for three hundred years; for all the modern scientific habit until that of yesterday proceeded from Descartes. He himself had no doubts upon the Faith, but his insistence upon the axiom that our acceptation of truth must depend upon external proof of it or upon deductive reasoning from observed constant natural "laws" did make profound inroads upon ordinary belief. It was from this attitude of mind that all that is called the "rationalistic" attack upon the Faith has ultimately grown.

Pascal had nothing to do with all this; he was right on the other wing, which bases religion on emotion. Protestantism, and particularly Calvinism—although Calvinism also is a strictly logical system—is based upon emotion. A religious truth is known to be true not on external evidence nor through deductive reasoning but because you have "experienced" it. Hence the typically Calvinist business of "conversion"—the sense of being "saved." Pascal, of course, did not accept such heresy, but he stood for a sort of compromise with it.

Now, after the vivid object lesson of the Reformation in action, men could see the danger of breaking with unity. But many of the most intense minds within the Catholic culture, and especially in France and what is called to-day Belgium, though they had a horror of Calvinism, were attracted to this factor of "religious experience," irritated by the constraints of an authoritative Church and its practice, which they found mechanical. Further, the great effect of the Jesuits had been to recover Europe for the Faith by making every sort of allowance—trying to understand and by sympathy to attract the worldly and the sensual and all the indifferent, and insisting the whole time on the absolute necessity of loyalty to the Church. Defend the unity of the Church, and talk of other things afterwards: preserve the Church which was in peril of destruction; only then, when you have leisure, after the battle, debate other things.

This being the Jesuit attitude, and the Jesuits having become by far the chief influence in the mid-seventeenth century throughout Catholic Europe, those men in Catholic Europe who leaned towards emotion in religion, towards personal experience, almost towards what the Calvinist enemy called "conversion," chose the Jesuits as their special antagonists. A powerful writer in the Netherlands called Jansen (in the Latin form Jansenius) stood for all this. He wrote a book based upon St. Augustine, and that book represented the reaction of Calvinism upon the Catholic

Church. Jansenism, as it was called, stood for all that swing, even in its extremes; and the great Pascal, a mathematician, as Descartes had been, but also what Descartes was not, a genius at writing, took up the cudgels for Jansenism. He did not know his subject well. He had to be coached. Most of what he wrote in his famous pamphlets the "Provinciales" shows ignorance of his authorities whom he only got at second hand. Also his puritanism could not survive. But his style had that principal effect which good writing always has, and by that he still lives.

From these two men, Pascal and Descartes, proceeded the two strains of influence which, between them, threatened to wreck the Catholic culture. Rationalism was its product, and first the deism and then the atheism of generations not yet born. Pascal and the Jansenists whom he defended acted as a support to the Huguenot revolt against the popular Church in their own country. The support was not fully conscious and never took the form of active rebellion, but it worked like a leaven throughout the generations to come, and went to swell the attack on the Faith which, spread so widely *in Catholic countries and especially France*, so threatened at last, two hundred years afterwards, during the nineteenth century, that till recently many thought the Church was doomed to decline and early extinction.

Meanwhile, two other things were at work which would also in the future militate against that Catholic culture in Europe by which alone civilization could be saved. The first was nationalism, and the second the growth in wealth and power of the anti-Catholic Protestant culture in the West.

Nationalism began, not in the worship of the nation, but in the worship of the Prince.

As in the case of Jansenism, the Catholic could not accept nationalism fully, but flirted with its ideas. Thus in the case of the all-powerful King-worship which is rampant all through the Reformation Period, the Catholic could not accept the full Protestant doctrine called the Divine Right of Kings. But those inclined towards this error went as near to it as they could, and the great exponent of such a king idol, of local civil claims encroaching on the universal authority of the Church, was *Louis XIV* of France.

He was a boy in the middle of the seventeenth century, he died several years after its close, he was the greatest power in all the latter half of that long lifetime of his. From, say, 1660 to 1715 *Louis XIV* meant more to the Europe of his time than, say, the British governing class to the Europe of the later nineteenth century. The king of France could never break with

Catholic unity, of course; indeed in a sense he was the champion of Catholicism, now that Spain (the old champion of Catholicism) was in decay and that France herself had broken the power of the Catholic German Empire. But though he was thus the champion of Catholicism he also went as far as he possibly could, short of breaking with the Holy See, in insisting upon the right of Princes to be independent within their own realms. As his realm was Gaul (or France) this spirit was called, on its religious side, Gallicanism. Out of this insistence upon independence by the Prince came the insistence upon the complete independence of nations, and that religion of patriotism which in our own time has grown to such exaggerated dimensions. Nationalism, the putting of the Nation (which is ourselves) in the place of God, is, indeed, the great heresy of our day.

Louis XIV, then, represented this force of separate independent national claims, disintegrating the Catholic culture from within. Meanwhile the House of Orange, especially, represented the force militating against the Catholic culture from without. And of the House of Orange, *William of Orange*, who usurped the English throne and was contemptuously allowed by the English wealthy families to replace the last Catholic and active King of England, was the outstanding figure. He was the contemporary of Louis XIV. He stood in England, and indeed throughout Europe, although he was not built on the scale for such a position, as the typical anti-Catholic political figure.

He was in England only a puppet King (under the title of William III). Men laughed at him and disliked him, but he was the symbol of the growing anti-Catholic power of money, trade and a new effort at expansion of commercial dominion over-seas, of which the Dutch had been the originators and of which the English were to be the heirs. Prussia, the great anti-Catholic force that was to come, had not yet been born.

With the typical figures here selected I shall to the best of my ability fill my gallery, taking in their order first the English figures of that foundational affair, the loss of England. Then in their order arise King Henry VIII, his Queen, Catherine, his Paramour, Anne Boleyn, his minister-master, Thomas Cromwell, Sir Thomas More, who withstood him, Thomas Cranmer, the King's ecclesiastical agent Gardiner, Clement VII, the Queens Mary and Elizabeth Tudor, Mary Stuart and the great William Cecil, Lord Burghley. So far the English Reformation on which all that was to follow turned.

I next describe the later men, the men of the seventeenth century, "The Drawn Battle" or stale-mate: Henry IV of France; then James I of England; then the Emperor Ferdinand, Gustavus Adolphus and Richelieu; then Laud, to illustrate the internal difficulties of Protestantism, which unfortunately did not prove fatal to it; then Oliver Cromwell. Then I shall consider Descartes and Pascal; lastly William of Orange, and Louis XIV.

KING HENRY VIII

HENRY VIII, who was King of England from 1509, when he was a lad of less than eighteen, to his death in 1547, is rightly regarded as the author of that great disaster the English Reformation. By this disaster the only one of the important districts of Europe which broke away from Christendom in the sixteenth century was turned against the general civilization of Europe. If England had not broken off, the Reformation would have failed and our civilization would have been to-day one Christian thing. It is impossible to exaggerate the importance of this historical catastrophe. It has had effects which have gone on spreading from that long distant date, more than 400 years ago, to our own time, and those evil effects are if anything increasing rather than diminishing.

There had begun in Germany a great revolt against Catholicism. It was the explosion of forces which had long been gathering, provoked by the divisions in the Church itself—the rivalries of Popes and anti-Popes—and the corruption in the hierarchy. This revolt broke out in 1517. It was wild and indeterminate in character. There was bound to come a reaction against it on the part of the forces of order, and Europe would have regained its religious unity had not England, much later in the story, broken away. England at the time when the trouble began in Germany was very little affected by heresy. King and people were quite normally Catholic.

The entry of England into the Reformation movement was an accident, the result of a side issue. This side issue was the desire of King Henry VIII to get an annulment of the marriage between himself and his legitimate wife Catherine, the daughter of the Spanish monarch. He wanted the marriage annulled because he had been completely captured by Anne Boleyn, a young woman of the Court, who would be satisfied with nothing less than being his Queen. He could not get the Pope to grant the annulment, so those who flattered and supported him and particularly his minister, Thomas Cromwell, gradually moved for the break with Rome. This was achieved at the end of 1534.

Henry tried to keep England Catholic without the Pope, but he failed, and after his death in 1547 the break-up of religion in England began. It was powerfully aided by the fact that Thomas Cromwell had urged the King to dissolve the monasteries and seize their wealth. But of this wealth the English landed classes, who were everywhere the local leaders, received the bulk, so that it was to their interest to further the Reformation, and it was this financial reason more than any other which worked unceasingly to drag England away from Catholicism.

Though so much else was at work, it will be seen that if Henry had not weakly allowed himself to be captured by Anne Boleyn, and then allowed himself to be pushed into the extreme position of breaking with the Papacy rather than disappoint the woman who had infatuated him, England would be Catholic to-day; and if England had remained Catholic the Reformation elsewhere would certainly have died out.

He it was who started the ball rolling. He did not intend the results which ultimately followed, nor even the results which followed immediately within his own lifetime, still less the results which followed after his death. It was a passionate, foolish, ill-considered blunder—and was a very good example of the truth that evil comes upon the world through men's blind sins much more than through their calculation.

To understand the character of Henry VIII one must begin by knowing what the England over which he ruled was like; how it stood among the nations, and what his own family was which had only recently arrived at the throne of England.

The England in which Henry was born in 1491 was a country of about four million inhabitants. Scotland was quite independent from it and regarded as a hostile country; the mountainous Welsh districts were not seriously governed by England, they were almost independent; so was Ireland, except for a rather narrow belt on the east coast with Dublin as its chief town. This country of four million inhabitants was only one of a number of provinces, so to speak, of Christendom, for all Christian Europe—Germany, Poland, Italy, the Scandinavias, France and Spain—were felt to be one thing and were, of course, united in religion under the Pope. The various Christian Princes and Free Towns and Commonwealths, though regarding themselves as independent one from the other, all felt themselves to be bound up in one great Catholic Commonwealth.

Of these various powers in Christendom the French kingdom (rather smaller than France is now) was the largest; Spain had recently been united by the marriage of the King of Aragon, Ferdinand, with the heiress of the

Kingdom of Castile, Isabella; Italy was broken up into a great number of city Republics and local sovereignties of which the Papal States, lying across the middle of the country, were the most important unit. Germany also was broken up into a great number of nearly independent lordships and cities, but over all of them was the Emperor who also had for his private kingdom Austria and the lands round about it.

There was a permanent rivalry between France and the German States and therefore the Emperor; and the way in which England (though a much smaller country) could play upon this rivalry had a great deal to do with her importance. In numbers and wealth England was then only about one fifth of France or of the German States, but she was defended by the sea (except on the northern Scottish border), was prosperous, and it made a great deal of difference to each of the rivals which side she took.

This England into which Henry VIII was born was agricultural; most of the towns were only market towns dependent upon the custom of the villages round about; there was only one really large city, London, with about 150,000 people. Norwich, which was the capital of the woollen industry, came next; and Bristol had a certain importance; but the great mass of Englishmen lived in the villages and by tilling the soil. It is important to remember this whenever one reads about the Reformation in England, because that movement was strongest in London and at first had hardly had hold in the countrysides. It was a foreign thing coming in through the seaports of which London was the greatest. If we remember this we can understand the apparent paradox that while foreign Ambassadors and other observers living in London speak of the growth of the Reformation the nation as a whole detests it and rises in rebellion against it.

The next thing to understand about the situation into which Henry VIII was born is that the King was everything. The political mood of men in those times took it for granted that one man ought to act for, and be responsible for, the community, and this one man not elected but possessing the throne of right by inheritance. The King was all-powerful, except, of course, that the Church was independent, and also that men were governed in those days by long-established custom which was the moral basis of law and which the King was supposed to support rather than to change. Parliaments were summoned from time to time to sit for a few weeks, but at irregular and often very long intervals; there was no idea of their governing but only of their being consulted to see whether extra money could not be provided for the King in times of crisis—for normally the King had to run the country on his own private income, which was, of course, enormous. Taxes as a permanent institution did not exist; they were levied only when there was some immediate and abnormal necessity for finding money for the government—usually on account of a war.

It must further be especially remembered that the family into which Henry was born had only just acquired the Kingship of England, and they were felt not only to be new-comers but (by many people) unlawfully possessed of power.

The ancient Kingship of England had been in the hands of the family called Plantagenet for hundreds of years. In the century before Henry was born the members of this royal family had quarrelled, the rightful King had been ousted and put to death by his cousin, and then there had been a reaction against the descendants of this usurping branch, and civil wars had followed between the various parts of the Plantagenet family for two generations; but still the Plantagenets were the reigning family, and everybody regarded them as the only true Royal blood with a right to govern.

It happened, about one long lifetime before Henry VIII was born, that the widow of one of the Plantagenet Kings, a French Princess, had secretly taken a lover of low birth, a Welshman employed about the Palace, called Tydder or Tudor—his obscure outlandish name was spelt and pronounced in various ways. Whether she was ever married to him we do not know, but probably she was not. However, her children by him, and especially the eldest boy, Edmund, were playmates to her own legitimate child by the late Plantagenet King her husband. And that child, of course, became later the King of England under the Plantagenet title of Henry VI. He showed great favour to his little base-born and probably illegitimate half-brother Edmund, and married him to a lady who was of Plantagenet blood though also, a couple of generations back, illegitimate.

These two, Edmund Tudor and his wife, had a boy called Henry, and this Henry Tudor—in the turmoil of the civil wars—became leader of one of the parties. He claimed the throne under the most shadowy rights, came over with a small army of Frenchmen to England from France where he had taken refuge, was supported by a good many of the nobility who hated the last Plantagenet King, Richard III, and with their help won the battle of Bosworth, where this last Plantagenet King, Richard III, was killed.

Henry Tudor then took the throne of England and started a new dynasty under the title of Henry VII. As he had hardly any claim, he strengthened his position by marrying the heiress of the Plantagenets. She was the niece of the last King (who had no children) and the daughter of the last King's brother, who had been King of England under the title of Edward IV.

All this happened in 1485, only six years before Henry VIII was born, so we see of what a new and unstable Royal family that child came.

Henry VII, the first Tudor King, and his wife had two sons as well as daughters. The elder son was called Arthur, and the second Henry (who became Henry VIII). Arthur was some years older than Henry and was the heir. In these two sons mixed two very different kinds of blood. The Queen, their mother, being the daughter of Edward IV—the handsomest man of his time—and her beautiful mother being of the fine Woodville family, handed on the strong physique, good health, vigour and the rest, of these families. On the Tudor side the blood was bad. Henry VII himself was frail and often ailing; he had been born too early in his mother's life and his mother's family was not remarkable for health either. It is important to remember this double strain in the children of the Tudors; it accounts for a great deal.

Henry VII negotiated a marriage between his heir, young Prince Arthur, and the daughter of Ferdinand and Isabella, the monarchs of Spain. She is known to history as Catherine of Aragon. They were only children of fifteen when the nominal marriage took place, it being celebrated thus early (as Royal marriages often were) in order to clinch an alliance; but Prince Arthur died immediately after the marriage, and we can be certain that it was never consummated. The poor young child Catherine, nominally widow of the last heir, was kept on at the English Court and a betrothal was arranged between her and her little brother-in-law Henry.

Betrothals in those days, and especially in that rank, were a very solemn affair, almost as binding as a marriage, and though the actual marriage could only take place when Henry should be grown up, yet even for the betrothal it was necessary to get a dispensation from the Pope of the day, Julius II, because Catherine had been (nominally at least) the wife of the boy's brother. It was a disputed point among theologians whether the Pope could or could not give a dispensation for marriage with a deceased brother's wife; morally, of course, it did not matter in this case because the marriage between young Prince Arthur and Catherine had only been a nominal one, but the point was to prove of enormous importance in the future.

Young Henry being thus left sole heir to the throne, his father died in the spring of 1509 some months before the boy would reach his eighteenth birthday. He duly succeeded under the title of Henry VIII, was crowned, and proceeded to marry at once this sister-in-law of his, Catherine, older than himself by nearly six years. They were at first very happy together, the young King was popular, his wife had an excellent influence over him, and everything went well.

Now let me describe the character of this young fellow, upon whom so much was to depend. His leading characteristic was an inability to withstand impulse; he was passionate for having his own way—which is almost the opposite of having strength of will. He was easily dominated, always being managed by one person or another in succession, from this beginning of his life to the end of it, but being managed—not bullied or directly controlled.

It is exceedingly important to understand this chief point about him because a misjudgment of it has warped much the greater part of historical appreciation upon him. Because he was a big man who blustered and had fits of rage and was exaggeratedly eager to follow appetite and whim he had been given the false appearance of a powerful figure. Power he had, but it was only the political power which the mood of the time gave to whoever might be monarch. He had no personal power of character. He did not control others by their respect for his tenacity, still less by any feeling that he was wise and just and still less by any feeling that he was of strong fibre.

On the contrary, all those who managed him, one after the other—except his wife—despised him, and soon came to carry on as though they could do what they liked on condition that they flattered him. They managed public affairs while he followed his appetites or private interests. That was true of the whole series of those who "ran" him: Wolsey, Anne Boleyn, Thomas Cromwell, and, at the end, his brother-in-law Seymour. The only exception was that admirable wife of his who, through the simplicity of her character and her strong affection as well as from her sense of duty, treated him with respect. But her influence over him was, perhaps on that very account, soon lost.

As might be expected with a nature of this kind, he revolted against each manager one after the other. He felt he was being "run" by each in turn, grew peevish about it, had explosions of anger and would in a fit of passion get rid of them. Getting rid of them often meant, under the despotic conditions of that day, putting them to death. That is how he suddenly broke with Wolsey, that is how he broke with Anne Boleyn, that is how he broke with Thomas Cromwell—who had all three done what they willed with him, acting independently of him, showing their contempt for him in private and ultimately rousing his fury. Every woman (except his first wife Catherine) with whom he had to deal treated him pretty soon with contempt, and that is a most significant test of a man's value.

He excelled during all the early part of his life in physical exercises; he was a first-rate rider, a good wrestler, a good shot, and until disease had quite wrecked his physique he could endure a good deal of fatigue. A big red-headed, broad-faced man with a sparse beard, somewhat pale eyes set far apart in a face at first ruddy, later rather pasty. He had an exaggerated fear of death and, what was inexcusable in a King of his generation, he would never risk his body in battle. He was terrified of epidemics, which were frequent in the crowded, ill-drained towns of that epoch, and he took precautions, often absurd, to avoid any chance of infection. There were moments when the fear of death was a positive monomania with him.

He was exceedingly intelligent, and well trained in theology, to which he had first been directed when, as a boy, it was not thought that he would ever be King and he was destined by his father to become ultimately Archbishop of Canterbury. He was also well-read, could speak several foreign languages, and could speak and even think in French, as was the custom in the better-instructed upper class of his time in all western countries and especially in England. It must be remembered that within a hundred years of his birth the English upper class spoke French only; English had only recently become the common tongue.

But though he was intelligent, in the sense of being able to follow a logical process clearly or to draw up a consecutive plan or to analyse intellectual propositions such as are presented by theological or political discussion, he was a bad judge of men. He could see indeed well enough that this man or that was working hard and producing results, but he blundered badly whenever he tried to frame a foreign policy for himself; also he was very hesitant—perhaps because he half consciously recognized his incompetence in dealing with a complicated situation.

He would put off a decision, advance towards a certain end and then draw back, half determining to give up objects towards which he was bent, and the main lines of action during his reign were always undertaken by somebody else.

It was Wolsey who conducted his early foreign policy entirely; it was Cromwell who later worked his breach with Rome; it was Seymour who, at the end of his life, determined what sort of will he should leave and how the succession to his throne should be arranged. He was emotional after a fashion, and especially sensitive to music; he was even a good practical musician himself and something of a poet and he composed a few songs which are not without merit, as well as other set pieces of harmony, notably two Masses to which are given his name but which are perhaps from his own hand.

He was very vain—vain of his looks, and of his athletics in early life; exceedingly touchy about his dignity and his majesty as a King. His feelings were here in comic contrast with the way in which he was always being got the better of by other people, until the moment when the regular explosion against their control arrived. It was this vanity which made him fall a victim to more than one woman, but it also prevented his being completely infatuated by them save in the one case of Anne Boleyn.

Was he industrious? The answer to this question must be as carefully sized as the answer to that other question we have already dealt with, the question of his strength. Just as he was certainly not really strong, so he was not really industrious in the sense of troubling himself to master a subject or a policy by concentrated application. He could never force himself to do things, he was much too much the slave of appetite and caprice for that. Yet one may call him industrious in the more superficial sense of the word, of getting through "agenda" and attending to what was put before him as a monarch. There is a vast mass of papers, many drawn up with his own hand, a great deal of annotation of documents with which he had to deal, which prove this quality in him. One cannot use for him the word "lazy." He did not simply leave all work to other people and forget it in amusements, but he had not in this any more than in other matters that control of himself; that grasp over his own activities, that power of compelling himself to do what he felt to be tedious, which is the mark of true industry; he did not *work* in the full sense of the word; he never got into the depth of anything he undertook to study or became the possessor of it.

Next we must specially insist upon the effect which time had upon his character—time and disease combined. At some date which we cannot exactly determine but certainly early in his life, probably well before his twenty-fourth year, he contracted syphilis. Thenceforward he gradually became a man deteriorating more and more in body and mind; he long retained his physical activity and to the end his mental activity, but he was more warped on the spiritual side until at last he became something of a monster—callous to the sufferings of others and capable of almost any cruelty in action. While on the physical side his health went all to pieces especially towards the end. For years the chief symptom of his troubles was a running ulcer in the leg, and for the last quarter of his reign he had become so huge, unwieldy and corrupt in person that he could hardly move. In the final years, though he was only a little over fifty, he had to be trundled about and his enormous bulk lifted in and out of a chair. At last he could not even sign his name; it had to be done for him with a stamp. But even to the very end he retained that sort of energy which takes its expression in violence.

He had, as might be imagined, very little power of self-restraint, and he never seems to have understood when this lack of control passed the bounds of common decency. Thus he would cry absurdly, almost like a child, especially when he was in a fit of passion or when he felt he had been made ridiculous.

Two last things must be mentioned about him, the first of which is very generally appreciated, the second of which is too often forgotten. The first is that his extreme selfishness, which grew upon him with the years, as selfishness always does in selfish men, probably passed at last the boundary of sanity, and this showed itself especially in the horrible acts of cruelty in the last part of his career. There had been plenty of cruelty in him when his character first began to deteriorate after Catherine lost her influence over him and after his disease had begun to work; but there were other political or personal reasons for it, while later it was often merely wanton and he would express, in the orders he gave, a sort of hellish savagery and greed of suffering and gloat over the agonies of his victims—such as those of the unfortunate Friar Forest whom he had roasted over a slow fire—and he mixed up horrors of this sort with the idea of grandeur. He seemed to think that they enhanced his stature in the eyes of his contemporaries and subjects. He came at last to rule by terror, and the extravagance of his later policy-such as the expedition to Boulogne—his sudden changes and his violent laws and edicts showed a crazy lack of balance.

But the second characteristic, most incongruous with such a character but undoubtedly present, was a strong attachment to the religious traditions in which he had been brought up. This was the only fixed thing in him approaching a principle. He destroyed or allowed to be destroyed the monastic institutions, which are the bulwark of the Church; he quarrelled and broke with the Papacy, which is the principle of unity in the Church (though in his time a principle confused and often debated); but he did have a fixed emotional attachment to the practices of the Faith, and he never got out of what may be called the atmosphere of these practices. He had a constant devotion to the Sacrament of the Altar and no little of his severity appeared in his treatment of anyone who denied the Real Presence. He insisted on the celibacy of the clergy, on the maintenance of full ritual in the liturgy and all ecclesiastical discipline under the episcopacy, which he formally maintained.

I have said that this side of him may appear incongruous with all the rest, and it is certainly strange in our modern eyes, but it is not so difficult to understand if we put ourselves in the position of his office and his time. He was sincere in these feelings, but his sincerity was reinforced by his vanity and by his constant insistence upon his political power. He thought of heresy under its aspect of rebellion, he disliked its variety and its anarchic quality because he lived by centralized despotism which he had inherited as a sixteenth-century King, and that very emotionalism which led him to his excesses of all kinds was capable of reinforcing him in those personal habits of worship which did not clash with his political objects.

There, as it seems to me, is the outline of the man. There is his character as a whole in all its lack of proportion and, as he developed, its grotesqueness. None could be better suited to produce the ill effects which it did produce. If the evil powers had had to choose their instrument, assigning to it the right proportions of violence and weakness, incomprehension, passion and the rest, they could hardly have framed a tool more serviceable to their hands than that which did—without full intention—effect the main tragedy in the modern history of Europe.

CATHERINE OF ARAGON

THE MARRIAGE of Henry VIII with Catherine of Aragon was of critical importance. Her age and character, the reactions of these upon Henry, her position in Europe and everything else connected with her, are of interest and moment to the understanding of the Reformation.

Catherine of Aragon was the daughter of two very remarkable people: Isabella, who on the death of her brother became heiress to the Kingdom of Castile, and Ferdinand who had been from early youth the King of Aragon. All the Spanish independent sovereignties had spread southward from the Pyrenees in the reconquest of the country from the Moors, who had overrun it in the high tide of Mahommedan enthusiasm in the century after Mahommed's own life-time. The chivalry of Christendom used to come volunteering year after year to join in the great struggle. They were rewarded by portions of the conquered lands; and ultimately the whole of what we call to-day Spain and Portugal—that is, the whole of the Iberian Peninsula south of the Pyrenees—had been reconquered for Christendom, except the southern strip round about the Sierra Nevada near the sea, called Andalusia, with its capital at Granada.

Aragon and Castile were the two main kingdoms of the Peninsula, and by the marriage of Ferdinand and Isabella all that land except Andalusia, which still remained to be reconquered, and Portugal (which had developed into an independent Christian Kingdom) were in one family. The marriage of Ferdinand and Isabella united Spain.

That marriage had taken place in 1460, and the Crowns were united after a Civil War in 1479. In 1492, the same year as that in which Columbus discovered America, but earlier in the year, the full conquest of the Peninsula was accomplished; the Mahommedan capital of Granada fell and the last shred of Mahommedan foothold in western Catholic Europe was destroyed. All this added greatly to the prestige of the now united Spanish Crown, and, of course, when it was appreciated what the discovery of America meant, that prestige rose higher still. When it was a little later appreciated what an immense wealth would come to the Spanish sovereigns from their claims in the New World, it rose higher again.

Hence, when Henry VII, with his base lineage and lack of claim—his haphazard acquirement of the English throne—arranged a marriage between his family and the Spanish Royal house, it was a very great thing indeed. There could be no comparison in the wealth or importance of the two.

Ferdinand and Isabella, "The House of Aragon," had a son who died before he could become King. They had also two daughters, Joan and Catherine. The latter was to become the wife of Henry VIII and Queen of England. Joan was of weak intellect and died probably quite deranged. She bears the nickname in history of "Joan the Mad." She was the elder and, therefore, able to transmit to her posterity the Kingdom of Spain. She was married into the highest family in Europe, the family of the Emperor.

The Emperor Maximilian, of the family of Hapsburg, having for private inherited domain the Arch-duchy of Austria and other lands adjoining, as well as what we now call Holland and Belgium and a great deal more in that district through a marriage with the heiress thereof, had a son, Philip, who would succeed his father in the sovereignty of all this great but scattered territory and probably—though not certainly—be elected Emperor after him. For a man became Emperor not by inheriting from his father but by election at the hands of the great magnates, lay and clerical, who governed principalities and dioceses among the Germanies; nor was he technically fully Emperor until he had been crowned by the Pope.

The office of Emperor was much the greatest in Europe, though it had no strong immediate political power, having no army of its own nor any revenue of its own, but depending upon the goodwill and support of the German Princes. However, in itself, to be Emperor was the greatest thing one could be; to marry the Emperor was the greatest marriage one could make. When, therefore, Joan of Aragon married Philip, this son of Maximilian, bringing with her the newly united Kingdom of Spain (which her children would inherit as her brother was dead), there was united (in prospect) under the rule of one man, Philip of Hapsburg, The Empire, and in direct rule large territories: including the immensely wealthy Netherlands with their great mercantile towns, southern Italy, which was part of the Crown of Aragon; and all Spain, with that new wealth which, it was now seen, was going to pour in from beyond the Atlantic.

It was a marriage which looked as though it would put into one hand much the greatest part of power in Europe. The only great country standing outside the combination was France. England was still inferior in numbers and wealth; Scotland smaller still; Portugal also small, Italy divided into various principalities; the Christian Empire of the East had gone down before the Mahommedan; Russia had not yet emerged. Hence it looked as though the family of Joan and Philip would overshadow all Christendom.

Philip died before his father Maximilian; and when Ferdinand of Aragon was dead and Isabella as well, the son of Philip and Joan, whose name was Charles, succeeded to his grandfather Maximilian. He, therefore, became Sovereign of Spain, and the new discoveries in America, and of the Netherlands and German Burgundy, and Austria, and all the rest; and, what was more, he was elected to the Empire as his grandfather had been, becoming Emperor in 1519.

The result of all this was that during Catherine's later years, when she was Queen of England and mother to the heiress of England, and later still when her husband was thinking of divorcing her, she was not only great politically, as the daughter of Ferdinand and Isabella, or as the wife of the King of England, but still more as the aunt, greatly revered and beloved, of Charles V, Emperor, and King of Spain, and far the greatest figure in Europe.

Catherine was born in December, 1485, the same year in which Henry VII had usurped the Crown of England by the lucky accident of the Battle of Bosworth. She was betrothed to the heir of this English King, bringing with her the *promise* of a large dowry. This young Prince was only fifteen years old, and, when he married Catherine, on November 14, 1501, she was not quite sixteen.

Here there are two things to be understood by a modern person to whom the conditions of that time are necessarily strange. First, Royal marriages of this sort between people who were still little more than children gave no scandal; they were a matter of course. Second, the question of a cash dowry was without question most important.

The reason for the first of these points was this; in the old united Christendom there were no wars of conquest properly so-called; Catholic morals did not admit the idea that any Christian prince was independent of the general scheme of Christian unity. He might put in a claim to a piece of territory, saying that he had a better right to its inheritance than the actual owners; he might fight to substantiate his claim, and no doubt his claim might be a flimsy one: but the modern idea of merely taking a thing by force from other Christians and then ratifying your theft by treaty occurred to no one.

The way in which States increased their powers or (as they would have put it) the way in which reigning families increased their powers, was by making marriages which would bring them in either large sums of money or new territories from which further taxes could be gathered. Therefore purely political arrangements were made by which quite young people, sometimes infants, were betrothed; the betrothal was not valid in the eyes of the Church, of course, until it had been ratified by the younger people after they had come to the proper age, but the two powers would hasten to have the marriage celebrated as soon as possible after the earliest canonical age allowed by the rules of the Church. Therefore young people of this rank were often married at such an age as saw the marriage of Catherine and Henry VII's heir, Prince Arthur. The marriage did not become a real marriage as a rule until somewhat later. All this must be borne in mind when we consider the case of Catherine of Aragon and Henry VIII's divorce from her.

This young Prince Arthur, younger even than his wife, died four and a half months after the marriage, on April 2, 1502; and young Catherine was left a nominal widow at the Court of her scheming father-in-law Henry VII, the Tudor King of England.

The next point to consider, for it was important, was the question of her dowry. Governments in those days did not spend, in proportion to the total national wealth, anything like the amount which they spend to-day; often they spent less than one fiftieth of what a modern Government will spend. There were hardly any national services; there was no national army, only a small bodyguard round the King; no real national navy, only a few ships belonging to the King and not kept up as a regular force. Most of the administration of the country was local, paid for and looked after by local lords; the cost of the administration of justice more than paid for itself by fines and fees; there were no permanent national debts.

An England of some four million people had a total wealth perhaps one twentieth of the modern wealth of England, and cost the Government no more than could be normally provided by the private income of the King; though that often had to be supplemented by all manner of expedients in the way of forced loans and, in times of strain—such as wars—by summoning national assemblies and begging people to give by way of exception—and not to form a precedent—sums of money to meet the difficulty of the moment. There were no regular taxes beyond the dues which men directly holding of the King paid to him as their lord and which, more or less generally, resembled customary—not competitive—rents.

The consequence of such a state of affairs was that comparatively small sums of money could make a great difference to any reigning family. Put in terms of modern money the private income of the King of England and all that he could get from his own estates (he was much the richest man in his own kingdom), from the waste lands and forests, and customs at the ports, and proceeds on the administration of justice, was not in modern money £2 a head of the population. Probably it was more like £1 a head, if that—even in the case of an exceptionally business-like and grasping monarch. Therefore a large cash dowry paid over on marriage into a foreign Royal family made a big difference.

Now Ferdinand and Isabella promised such a large dowry with their daughter Catherine, but they could not pay it all at once. There was a debt owing, and this had two important consequences. In the first place it made Henry VII of England anxious, in spite of his son's death, to keep the money which he already had of the dowry and to keep his claim for the balance; in the second place it gave him a hold upon the Kingdom of Spain and made him secure in his alliance with that power.

Hence the betrothal between young Catherine and Arthur's little brother Henry, now the heir to the throne, who was later, on his father's death, to become Henry VIII. A dispensation was required of course, because it was neither affirmed nor proved that the marriage between Catherine and Arthur had not been consummated. There was a good deal of debate, as we have seen in talking of Henry VIII, upon whether the Pope could give such a dispensation; that is, upon whether the prohibition against marrying a deceased brother's wife were a matter of Divine or of human law, since, of course, the Pope cannot dispense from Divine Law. However, the dispensation was obtained from Pope Julius II in 1504; and after Henry VII's death young Henry VIII, then a few weeks short of his eighteenth birthday, married Catherine. She was five and a half years his senior, but still quite young. They had been brought up together and Henry was delighted with, and determined on, the marriage.

In the interval between Arthur's death and her marriage with Henry, Catherine had had a very difficult time. She could not speak English, her French was doubtful, her native Castilian was the only tongue in which she could think or express herself readily. She had but one close friend to remind her of home—a Confessor of the same nationality as herself, and she was told not to be too intimate with him. Her wretched father-in-law, Henry VII, had proposed at one moment to marry her himself, and even got the unfortunate child to write a letter saying that she was willing; but the indignant protest of her mother Isabella put an end to that project at once.

Her marriage with young Henry, therefore, was a relief, and, as he was at that moment, it was also a delight. She was very fond of him as he was of her. But she was unselfish, whereas he was already one of the most selfish young men alive. The difference in age, which had not yet affected Henry's feelings, gave her a yet stronger feeling of affection, a protective feeling for him, and he was greatly under her influence.

In person Catherine was short, broad and fair. Active enough in body, she had one very pleasing mark, which was a charming temper; she was friends with everybody and always smiling; universally popular and at the same time busy in all her employments as Queen. She was thoroughly liked by her subjects and by everyone about the young Court. She was pious, as for that matter was Henry too, after his fashion, but she was more rigid and austere in her Spanish piety.

She had one defect in the business of governing, which was a virtue in itself and would have been an advantage in any other position, though it was a disadvantage in the position of Queen. She was very simple. It went with being very direct and straight-forward; but she could not understand intrigue, she did not trouble to sound people's motives, she was rather too easily taken in. Over and over again during her life she acceded to proposals which would have been to her disadvantage and from which wiser and more corrupt people had to dissuade her. But she was industrious and looked well after any affair that she undertook, and her servants and dependants were devoted to her. She ruled her household well.

She acted as Regent while her young husband was away at the wars in France; she was responsible for the great victory of Flodden five years after her marriage. Had Henry continued to receive her influence throughout the remainder of his life it would have been well for both of them, and especially would it have been well for England.

In active affairs all that Henry did, especially in foreign policy, was more and more managed by Wolsey, the great cleric and statesman who took over the government of the kingdom and whom Henry wholly followed. But Catherine did not clash with Wolsey; she quite understood how superior was his intelligence and energy and what great capacities he had for holding the helm of the State. The trouble between her and her husband which broke her heart and made of the whole of her life so great a tragedy came from two things:

First of all, it came from the wretched instability of Henry's character—

sensual, capricious, unable to control appetite and abominably indifferent to the sufferings of others—spoilt in every way and spoilt, I am afraid, not a little by Catherine herself, who had made no effort to check him in spite of her affection.

Secondly, it came from her bad health, or at any rate her misfortunes in the matter of children. It is true that the King's own debauchery was responsible for her health later on, but I doubt whether it was responsible for it in the first year of the marriage. We have no direct proof, of course, one way or the other, but it seems unlikely from all we know of his actions and appearance when Henry first married her that he was not then a healthy man. But later she had miscarriage after miscarriage, and still-born child after still-born child. Only one child survived; Princess Mary, born in February 1516. There was no son and no other surviving issue when, five years later, it was known that Catherine could bear no more children. That was round about 1521–22.

Now here arises an important point. To what extent was Henry influenced in the abominable thing he did by the desire for an heir? Did his wronging of Catherine have any excuse in his disappointment at having only a daughter to succeed him?

The white-washers of Henry and the defenders of the great tragedy of the Reformation have argued with all their weight on that side. They have pretended in different degrees of sincerity that Catherine's ill success in providing him with an heir is the root of the affair. Not one who reads the contemporary documents of the time can believe that.

The root of the affair was Henry's miserable infatuation with Anne Boleyn. But the first duty of the historian is to be just; and we must allow a certain weight to Henry's desire for a male heir. These things cannot be put in exact proportion or percentages, but if one attempts to put it thus and give the disappointment at the lack of an heir from one fifth to one quarter of his motive, one may perhaps roughly represent the weight which it bore.

He was somewhat worried by not having a male heir because his throne was not too stable; his father had been a usurper and only captured the throne twenty-four years before his son's accession. It was in its way important to leave a son to carry on the dynasty; on the other hand the greatest thrones in Europe were handed on through women—Spain itself was a splendid example—and the little Princess Mary was so popular with everyone and would have been so thoroughly supported that there was no real danger.

Put forward as the main excuse for the divorce, the pretence that the necessity for a male heir was the leading motive was falsehood and hypocrisy.

When it was clear that Catherine could bear no more children, Henry gradually deserted her. He had several affairs; he took up with a woman whom he had known in boyhood—one Blount—and had a son by her whom he called the Duke of Richmond. He also took up with the daughter of a courtier and diplomat of his called Boleyn, a young lady of the name of Mary, and when he was tired of her he married her off to one of his other courtiers with a portion which did no credit to his generosity.

He probably ceased to live with his wife as early as 1521, when he was no more than thirty, and she, poor woman, still under thirty-seven. Even by his own admission (and he was a great liar) he ceased to live with her within the next three or four years.

It was about 1522 that he first noticed Anne Boleyn, the sister of Mary, probably with the object of making her his mistress. And it was probably about 1525 that they came to some arrangement together to try and get rid of Catherine and conclude a marriage. The first document dealing with the divorce is dated 1526, when Catherine was forty-one years old and Henry thirty-five. The first open steps taken for obtaining the divorce were in the next year, 1527.

During all these half dozen years of strain and contumely, Catherine bore herself with admirable dignity and restraint—probably with too much restraint. She might have done better had she protested, for Henry still stood in some fear and respect of her, and though he was passionate and would have outbreaks when he was thwarted he was, like nearly all sensual men, subject to the control of stronger characters than himself.

But Catherine made no attempt at any such control, though Anne Boleyn was one of her Maids of Honour, closely attached to her train at Court. She neither made scenes, nor intrigued to recover her position. What she did do was to remain absolutely steadfast in her determination that her husband should never have it in his power, so far as she could prevent it, to call any other woman wife and Queen.

On that she was inflexible, and the very simplicity of her character lent her strength. As the shameful efforts against her legitimate position increased in violence, when Wolsey had lent himself to the plan, when all Europe was discussing it and was concerned with the fate of the Queen of England, she remained immovable and almost silent.

She depended, of course, almost entirely upon the advice of her nephew, the Emperor Charles V; his Ambassador was her chief Councillor; she did all by his advice. There, again, perhaps she was too docile or too humble.

She might have attempted more on her own initiative, for it must be remembered that the Emperor had many political ends to serve; he needed Henry's help against the rivalry of France, and his Ambassador would often misjudge English affairs.

Her policy therefore may not always have been directed on the lines best calculated to succeed; but she had what is better than policy, a perfectly clear principle; and a rigid attachment to it has made her name stand as high as it can, from those days to our own.

What is more remarkable, she preserved the esteem and somewhat shamefaced regard of Henry. Even when he had refused to see her any more, probably because he was still afraid of her influence and did not like to look her in the face—when he had announced that she was no longer to be called Queen, but only Princess Dowager; when he had had her divorced in spite of the Pope by Anne Boleyn's man Cranmer (who had been made Archbishop of Canterbury for the sole purpose), she remained exactly the same.

She claimed her full title, she refused to admit the right of the court to examine her marriage with Arthur, she equally maintained the right of her daughter to be heiress to England; and when Boleyn had the child Elizabeth, in September 1533—illegitimate in the eyes of all Europe and by all Christian law—the people of England steadfastly continued to regard Catherine as the legitimate Queen, and Princess Mary as the right inheritor of the throne.

She did not long survive the tragedies which had been imposed upon her, and which she had borne with such steadfast courage. She died in January, 1536, too early to see the fall and disgrace of her rival, Anne Boleyn; and almost her last act was a letter still full of passionate love written to the King, who had not allowed her so much as to see him for now more than six years. It was then she wrote the famous phrase, "The desire of my eyes is to see you again." But the man had damned himself.

They buried her in Peterborough Cathedral, not putting over her one of those great and splendid tombs of the Renaissance, such as all her high kindred had throughout the West, but a plain slab of black stone on which there was not even an inscription till modern times. One may meditate with some profit on that simple and ignominious piece of masonry, the poor tomb of so good a woman who stood at the origin of such great and disastrous things.

It was widely believed, and on good authority, that her rival had caused her to be poisoned. It is equally probable, perhaps more probable, that she died a natural death; for we know from the autopsy that there was a small growth upon her heart which may have been cancerous.

She died, as her daughter Mary was to die many years later, hearing Mass, the Mass that was said in her sickroom. She made the responses and received Holy Communion. And it is memorable, and typical of her Spanish rigidity and orthodoxy as well as of her training in Catholic things, that when her Chaplain and Confessor offered to say Mass for her before the Canonical hours lest she should die without it, she bade him wait until the regular time had come—and she lived on the few hours sufficient to enjoy the fruits of her patience.

ANNE BOLEYN

ANNE BOLEYN is the pivot figure of the English Reformation. It was through her that the political and social phenomenon called Protestant England came into the world.

She was not, of course, the cause of the movement, still less the cause of its final result. Innumerable causes converged toward that. But the movement would not have been launched, would not have been directed towards the goal which it ultimately reached, had not Anne Boleyn so completely dominated the King of England as to compel him ultimately to break with the unity of Christendom; and though Henry remained deeply attached to the Catholic doctrine and practice until his death, once he had broken with unity—that is, with the Papacy—there was a breach in the dyke and the flood was ready to pour through.

Not only was Anne Boleyn not the cause of the great affair, but still less was she the inspirer of it. Least of all the actors, with the exception perhaps of Henry himself, was she filled with any conscious intention of effecting such a result. The personality to whom must be given that role of inspirer, the mind which planned the origins of that great change and made it likely to succeed through economic as well as religious policy, was the mind of Thomas Cromwell.

Anne, then, was neither, the cause nor the inspirer of the first movement away from Catholicism. But she is what I have called her, the pivot figure. It is because she was what she was, and did what she did, that England is what England is to-day.

It is, therefore, of the first importance to history to understand what this woman really was and the real place of her action in the whole scheme of the time. From her day to our own it has been taken for granted by all national tradition and by every historian that she lay at the origins of the English Reformation, but latterly there has arisen an effort to weaken or question this sound tradition and to explain in other ways the quarrel between Henry and Rome and the ultimate effect of it. This effort at supplanting true history by false is part of the general scepticism of our time, which is usually ready to accept anything new because new falsehoods sound more picturesque as a rule than well-worn truths. But there is here a more powerful motive, to make the origins of the change of religion in England look a little less ignoble than they really are. That is why Professor Pollard, for instance, who is the chief authority on the details of the period in England, tries to maintain the fantastic theory that Henry's attempt to get rid of his wife was not connected with Anne Boleyn, but with larger reasons of State, and that he had had the policy of getting rid of Catherine of Aragon in mind for many years before he met Anne Boleyn. The idea is not only fantastic, but desperate; it has no chance of being accepted out of England, and I do not think it will be accepted even in England save by those who are very hard up for material in the whitewashing of Henry VIII's character.

No, Anne remains and will always remain at the origins of the catastrophe. It behoves us therefore to understand her and her effect as best we can.

Anne Boleyn was a Howard. That is the first thing to grasp in connection with her, and it is all the more important to grasp it because historians have failed to stress as strongly as they should have stressed this capital feature in her position. She was a Howard through her mother, who was the daughter of that old Duke of Norfolk, the victor of Flodden, and who was the sister of his son Thomas, third Duke of Norfolk, who played a great part throughout the whole of Henry VIII's reign.

The Howards were semi-royal. They had a somewhat different character from all the other great English nobles, although the family was not remarkably old, and the reason of this particular character of theirs was that they stood for a younger branch of the Plantagenet family, which was the true blood royal of England. The greatest of the Plantagenet kings, Edward I, one of the chief figures of the height of the Middle Ages, the contemporary of St. Louis, and of Alphonse of Castile, and of St. Dominic, had a young son, Thomas, generally called Thomas of Brotherton. He gave him vast estates, the title of Norfolk and the hereditary post of Earl Marshal of England—that is, head of the English armed forces. The family of this Thomas soon ended in an heiress, who married a Mowbray, whereupon her husband took on the title of Earl Marshal and all the tradition of the younger Plantagenet branch.

The Mowbrays again soon ended in an heiress, who married a wealthy private gentleman of legal descent, but one already possessed of land in East Anglia. This private gentleman was called Howard, and his son took over the tradition of Thomas of Brotherton and of the Plantagenet younger line. He was hereditary Earl Marshal of England through this marriage, and he was made Duke of Norfolk—the title of Duke being at that time of quasi-royal significance and only given to those who were of royal blood or represented a branch of it. In Anne Boleyn's time the Howard marriage into the Blood Royal was already more than a century old.

This Howard who thus became Duke of Norfolk only acquired his title thirty years before Henry VIII came to the throne, and, though they were not, under the name of Howard and through the male line, of any great importance, they were very important as representing the continued tradition of the Earl Marshalship and the younger Plantagenet blood and as having a Dukedom with its connotation of connection with the Crown.

This first Duke of Norfolk had fought against Henry VIII's father, and his title had been taken away from him, but it was restored to his son—the one who was victor at Flodden, as I have said—who was called the second Duke of Norfolk; and it was inherited by his son, again Thomas, third Duke of Norfolk, the uncle of Anne Boleyn.

So Anne Boleyn comes to the court of Henry VIII under the introduction and auspices of the Howard connection.

Her father, Sir Thomas Boleyn, was a very wealthy man, nothing like the equal of his wife socially, but of considerable family importance through *his* mother, of the Irish family of Ormonde. On his father's side he was descended from big merchants in the City of London. He had considerable talent, especially as a diplomatist, and was used by the Government on many occasions.

Now that we have understood who Anne Boleyn was in the high society of England at the time, the next thing to understand is her age, appearance and character.

Oddly enough (considering what a great position she held even before captivating Henry) we are not quite certain of the date of her birth. It would take up too much space to marshal all the arguments here which have been advanced for various dates; the one most generally given, 1507, is almost certainly wrong. I myself incline to 1502 or 1503; at any rate it was earlier rather than later. The point is of importance, because her age has a good deal to do with our understanding of the way in which she intrigued and of her capacity for fulfilling her ambition. If she were born in 1507, she would be only eighteen when Henry began to understand that he could not have her unless he married her, and she would only be fourteen when she is first talked of as mixed up in an affair. That is why 1507 seems to me an impossible date, for men were already claiming to be her lovers as early as 1521. On the other hand, if she were eighteen in 1521 and over twenty when she began to make it clear to Henry that he must marry her and that she would not be his mistress, the whole state of affairs becomes explicable.

Anyhow we may take it that round about the year 1525 this young woman was something between twenty and twenty-three years of age and had thoroughly captured the King. She was about the court both as the daughter of her important official father and as an attendant upon the Queen Catherine, but also in another connection which it is important though unpleasant to recollect, because it helps to explain Henry's action. Her younger sister Mary had already been the mistress of Henry VIII in very early youth, and he had got rid of her by marrying her off to one of his gentlemen. (She is usually called the older sister, but this is a mistake.)

Anne's appearance was singular. She carried herself rather badly, was flat-chested and round-shouldered. She had a very thin neck, with the Adam's apple prominent and large—to which it was thought she owed her really fine contralto voice. She also had very long dark glossy hair and powerful black eyes. Beautiful in any ordinary sense of the word she certainly was not. But she had a strange and not healthy power of fascination, at least over certain types of men. She was slightly deformed. The little finger of one hand was double. Those who would flatter her called it "two nails." People on the other tack roundly said that she had two little fingers. It was a defect which she was always at pains to conceal as best she could.

She used her fascination calculatedly and coldly, and she so used it from a very early age. When she may have been anything between her sixteenth and her eighteenth year—more probably about eighteen—in the year 1521 she so caught and entangled the heir of the greatest non-royal family in England, the Percys of Northumberland, that he was hopelessly in her power. He remained till his death full of that memory, long after he had had to give her up; for when she found she had a chance of higher game she got rid of him at once.

Meanwhile she had had a second string to her bow, even at that early period, in another conquest of hers, Wyatt, a gentleman closely connected with Henry, not a pleasant character and one who later, I think, traduced her, pretending that she had been his mistress as quite a young girl. I do not think this is true, because of what we know of Wyatt's character and what we know of her own, which was frigid and determined to make the most of every opportunity. There was nothing impulsive about her. She would not have ruined her chances by yielding to a man in Wyatt's position.

It was probably as early as this time, 1521, that the King, who was then a man of thirty, began to consider her. He probably also had about that time, and certainly immediately afterwards, given up living with his legitimate wife, Catherine, although there was no outward semblance of any breach between them. He had already had other adventures, and that illegitimate son borne to him by Elizabeth Blount, a lady who had been an old playmate of his in early youth. We have seen also how he had taken Anne's sister Mary for a mistress and discarded her. I have said that this point should especially be borne in mind, because it helps to explain the way in which Anne, who seems to have had much more will power than her sister, attracted him. He was evidently drawn to the family type.

We must presume, of course, that Henry at this early stage did not intend marriage. He sent sharp orders that the engagement with young Percy should be put to an end and used Wolsey as his agent in so doing. Some think, however, that he was thus acting as early as 1521 rather with the idea of making a marriage for Anne as heiress of the Ormondes and thus using her politically. Whether this were so or no, at any rate soon after he intended to make her his mistress.

We have no documents; we can only judge by the nature of the case and by what followed. But it is fairly clear that some time before, or in the very early part of 1525, when Henry was thirty-four years of age, and Anne well over twenty, perhaps as much as twenty-three, there was some arrangement between them, and that Anne had already given Henry to understand that she would not be his mistress, but would envisage marriage if he could get rid of Catherine. In that year her father was raised to the peerage and given a new and more prominent position, and in that year we have also large gifts from Henry to Anne, and Henry interfering with her movements and saying where she is to stop.

It does not follow that Henry had thus early accepted the idea of marrying Anne. He probably still thought she would become his mistress at last. To attempt the repudiation of Catherine, the niece of the Emperor of Germany and the King of Spain, the most prominent woman in the greatest family in Europe, would be a very serious business indeed, and Henry's hesitating and uncertain character would hardly come to a decision at once in the matter.

In the summer of 1526 he had taken the first steps towards getting the marriage with Catherine annulled, upon the plea that the original dispensation for marrying his deceased brother's wife was invalid. In 1527 he took open steps in this direction and for the divorce, as it was called, though of course it was an effort at annulment and not at divorce in the modern sense of the term—for in those days when everybody was Catholic divorce in the modern sense was not conceivable. And thenceforward for five years Anne tyrannized over him more and more, until the unfortunate man was hardly sane in regard to her. She could do what she willed with him and drove him at her discretion to the most impossible public actions. In order to get her, he began that worrying of the Pope which ended at last in the complete breach with Rome.

What exactly the relations were between them during this interval we can guess rather than prove, though even our guess must be of a tentative character, as it is also of a displeasing one. Displeasing though it be, it is necessary to have some precision in the matter, because unless we appreciate the relations of these two, we shall not understand the complete subjection into which Henry fell.

She would not allow him complete satisfaction until she was virtually certain—every obstacle having been removed by the death of the old, very Catholic and saintly Archbishop Warham—that even if the Papal court did not grant annulment, Henry would take the matter into his own hands and marry her.

She thus began to live with Henry as though she were already married to him, somewhere about September or October of the year 1532. Before Christmas of that year she was with child. Her chaplain, Cranmer, had been marked down for the Archbishopric of Canterbury; he was enthroned in the March of 1533, pronounced the marriage between Henry and Catherine null and void, proclaimed Anne to be the legitimate wife of Henry immediately after, and crowned her Queen in Westminster a few days after the sentence. Her child, who grew up to be Queen Elizabeth, was born in the September of that year.

Now began the process which may be observed in parallel cases in all times and places, including our own day. It was a case such as many of us have come across in our own observation. Henry having been driven pretty well off his head by this woman's pertinacious handling of him and refusal for so many years to surrender herself completely to him, was, now that he obtained satisfaction, changed in her regard.

She had a bitter tongue, not without wit, using the French language, in which she was trained and in which she thought as well as spoke. She ridiculed Henry behind his back, and he got to hear of it. Her fine voice in singing had ceased to attract him—perhaps it had also deteriorated. She had accumulated enemies by her violent fits of temper, which she had never restrained in her angers with Henry himself. So it was not only the weariness of Henry with her, but also active irritation against her, which began to change her fortunes. He was tired of her, he began to dislike her, soon he hated her; and if they still carried on, it was only because Henry hoped that she would give him an heir, a boy.

She probably would have done so but for his brutality, for a miscarriage which she suffered early in 1536 was by herself ascribed to his infidelity and roughness to her. She said she had been so pulled down by the whole business that her health had suffered: and we must remember in this connection that Henry himself had long been suffering from venereal disease.

At any rate, a miscarriage she had, and what with his disappointment and his increasing loathing, Henry was determined to be rid of her. His character had deteriorated rapidly; moreover he was superstitious, and seems to have got it into his head that she had bewitched him. An indictment was framed against her, the validity of which I will discuss in a moment. She was accused of adultery with various people, including a couple of gentlemen about the court, one of the royal musicians, of lower birth, and even with her own brother.

Thomas Cromwell, then all-powerful, master of things spiritual and temporal in England, as the King's viceregent over his new schismatic church, and the King's lieutenant in civil affairs, was as determined as Henry upon her death, for it would get rid of a rival. Henry had already determined who should succeed her, a certain Jane Seymour, daughter of a small landed gentleman in Wiltshire, whose sons were employed at court, while Jane herself was, as Anne had been, about the Court as a maid of honour.

Henry and Cromwell used Cranmer to ruin Anne, by frightening and threatening her after a pretended friendship, and Cranmer's action was the more base considering that his whole advancement and position were solely due to his having been a creature of the Boleyns and their chaplain. The wretched woman fell into an hysterical condition at the approach of death; she was left uncertain whether she would be burned or decapitated. On Friday, May 19, 1536, she was beheaded with a sword within the precincts of the Tower of London, by the headsman from Calais, specially brought over for the execution.

Was she guilty of the misconduct ascribed to her? It is one of the most fiercely debated points in English history. Standing as she does at the origins of the Reformation, the favourers of that movement have been hot in her defence. On the other hand, those who desire to exculpate Henry as much as they can exculpate that detestable character, like to believe her guilty, while for the defenders of the old Religion nothing was too bad to be put down to Anne.

The accusations, especially that of incest, seem so monstrous that their very enormity is an argument in her favour. On the other hand, she was certainly unscrupulous in affairs of this kind, and she seems to have been quite unbalanced in the last year or two of her life. Some who have medical experience in these matters maintain that she suffered from a particular irresponsibility, which makes the charges credible enough. I have myself always inclined to accept them. But many good students of the period with whom I have discussed the matter are divided, and some urge the strong argument that the two gentlemen concerned did not confess, while the musician, who did, confessed only under threat of torture. Anyhow, they were all put to death as well as herself.

Catherine had died before her. Henry's marriage with Jane Seymour which took place immediately after Anne's death was therefore quite legitimate in the eyes of the Church, and quite probably there would have been a reconciliation with Rome had it not been for Thomas Cromwell's having already launched the policy of confiscating church property, beginning with the monasteries, a policy which created a vested interest of great power against re-union.

Anne's fatal action, therefore, had come just sufficiently late to start the ball of the Reformation rolling. She had not intended it, she had intended only to fulfil a petty and personal policy, in which she triumphed only to bring about her own destruction. But she will remain for ever, in spite of lack of intention, the origin of that long movement which ended by the complete change of the English mind and character and the supplanting, after a troubled and heavily contested struggle lasting over a hundred and fifty years, of the old Catholic England by the new and modern Protestant one.

THOMAS CROMWELL

THOMAS CROMWELL is one of those figures in history, not numerous, of which we may say that they are never presented in their full stature.

He was, in his own line, a genius of the first order, and fortune allowed him to play a part of the first magnitude. He is the true creator of the English Reformation, and therefore of the general catastrophe which overwhelmed the secure and ancient civilization of Christendom.

Yet for a dozen men who could tell you a fair amount about his master, Henry VIII, or about any other of the prominent figures of the time there is barely one who could give you much more than the name of Thomas Cromwell, or, perhaps, add to it the fact that it was he who undertook the destruction of the English monasteries.

What is still stranger, most people do not connect him with the other famous Cromwell, Oliver, though Oliver was his great-nephew. But there is a reason for that: it has always paid the official historians in England (and pretty well all English history of the modern sort is official and anti-Catholic) to pretend that Oliver Cromwell was a bluff middle-class person truly representative of the English people, and to conceal the fact that he was the cadet of an immensely wealthy family, one of the wealthiest in England, whose huge fortunes came entirely from the loot of the Church.

What adds to one's estimate of Thomas Cromwell's intellectual stature, and one's corresponding detestation of the harm he proved capable of doing, is the fact that he was the sole architect of his own fortunes. Alone of the principal Reformation figures he started from nothing: no birth, no money, no classical or clerical education, no friends—nothing.

He was the son of a petty beer-house keeper in Putney. When he had grown famous and powerful stories grew up about him, of course, as they always will about such people, but when you look into them you find that the only certain fact is what I have just stated: his coming from this beer shop on the south bank of the Thames, a little above London.

He went off as a vagabond in early youth, and the very little we know of him seems to show that he took what was then the best chance for an adventurous tramp—military service. He seems to have hired himself out to some one of those captains who went about gathering fighters for hire and then striking a bargain with the various princes and powers at war; for in those days there were no standing armies, and no conscription, and when Governments wanted to fight they had to raise what men they could hurriedly and at fairly high pay.

The best field for this kind of thing was Italy, and thither young Cromwell drifted. Probably he got some loot out of the fighting; but also pretty certainly picked up some Italian, for he read Machiavelli and in later life would quote his maxims.

With whatever little capital he had got together in this dangerous trade he appears in the house of some big Italian money-lenders of the day; later on he returned to England and started on his own as a money-lender, on quite a large scale.

But Thomas Cromwell was much more than a moneylender, even in those first years of his advancing manhood. He had got hold of a good deal of law, and he had a fine grasp of detail in all business, remarkable industry, lucidity of judgment and rapidity of action. It was these which recommended him to the notice of the great Wolsey. He may have been recommended by one of the many fairly important people to whom he had lent money and whose bonds he held—for the money-lender can always get recommendations at the expense of relieving his debtor a little from pressure.

Anyhow, he appears as a sort of manager for Wolsey in important affairs, and so gets richer and richer. Unfortunately for Cromwell's soul, and for the Catholic Church in England, and indeed throughout Christendom, he happened to come into Wolsey's employ just at the moment when the great Cardinal was planning his new and splendid college at Oxford, which was to be something much bigger than the University had yet known.

In order to found this College, Wolsey had got the Papal authority to suppress a certain number of small decayed monasteries, draft the monks into the larger houses of their Orders and use their revenues for this great new establishment of his, which would also, of course, be of a clerical character. In visiting the smaller monasteries, whose wealth was thus transferred to another kind of clerical use, Wolsey employed Thomas Cromwell. And it was in these visitations that Cromwell learned all the technique of visitation and enquiry and inventory, and all the rest of it.

When Wolsey fell, after Henry's failure to obtain a divorce from Rome, Thomas Cromwell played a very clever game. He boldly sought an interview with the King, the details of which are, of course, hidden, but the results of which are clear, and of which Henry's cousin Cardinal Pole has told us the essentials. He seems to have urged upon the King the policy of *threatening* the Pope with schism unless the divorce were ultimately granted. And perhaps at the same time he made the first suggestion of looting the Church.

But, though he thus went over to the secret service of the King, he was not publicly admitted to be a royal servant till nearly three years later. He was not so foolish as to throw over Wolsey, his late master. In the first place, he knew very well that nothing would make him look more odious than ingratitude. In the next place, there was nothing to be gained by spurning the great man who had made his career, and in the third place, what I think decided him, he knew that Henry in his heart regretted the loss of Wolsey.

The King had been compelled by Anne Boleyn to get rid of Wolsey, but he would send, semi-privately, messages to the fallen minister and felt a continued real friendship for him; so it would never have paid Thomas Cromwell to have given Henry the impression that he, Cromwell, was Wolsey's enemy. However, Wolsey died soon after, and therefore that part of the problem was solved.

Cromwell continued through the successive years of the divorce movement—that is, 1531, 1532 and 1533—to frame and urge the governmental policy and to increase the pressure on the Pope. He was, for instance, the author of that special piece of policy called the Annates Bill.

The Annates were the first year's revenue of any Bishop's See in England, which was paid over to the Papal Court as a tax. A new Bishop on being appointed to a See paid over the first year's revenue in this fashion to Rome. Cromwell had a law made saying that the Annates were to be henceforward payable not to Rome but to the King's treasury, *but adding that whether this law should come into effect or not depended upon the King's good will.*

The object was, of course, to put an increasing strain upon the Papal policy. If the Annates had been confiscated, the Papal treasury would have had no cause to bargain, but with the *threat* of confiscation hanging over the Pope's head, it was hoped that he would prove amenable to Anne Boleyn's desire and pronounce Henry's marriage with Catherine null and void.

In the same way it was Thomas Cromwell who pushed through the final steps of the schism, ending with the decisive act of November, 1534, when Henry was declared Head in all things, spiritual and temporal, of the Realm of England, with power to judge in all spiritual cases and to define doctrine and the rest of it.

Cromwell made of his master Henry a local lay Pope. And how true this is you can see from the fact that Henry insisted on Papal titles being given to himself; he called himself the Vicar of Christ on earth so far as the Realm of England was concerned and had formulas used to him which were the same as those hitherto used to the Pope by those who addressed him official letters.

Thomas Cromwell by the time all this was accomplished—that is, by the time Cranmer had pronounced the divorce between Henry and Catherine of Aragon, by the time Henry had married Anne Boleyn, by the time Anne Boleyn's child, Elizabeth, had been born and declared heir to the throne—was completely master of England and wholly controlled and managed Henry himself.

Cromwell was not only the lay head of the country—a despotic minister with absolute power doing what he willed—but he was also the spiritual head, for Henry delegated to him all his own spiritual power. And Cromwell exercised that spiritual power very thoroughly indeed. He made the Bishops understand that they were nobodies compared with himself, he sent his officials throughout their dioceses adjudicating and settling and punishing and the rest, as though he were a universal bishop whose power superseded that of all others. Yet all the time Cromwell was only a layman.

Within a year of Cromwell's having worked the schism with Rome— that is, in 1535—he began two things side by side. One was a reign of terror, which was inaugurated by the arrest and at last the execution of very highly placed people, laymen and clerics, who withstood the schism; the other was the dissolution of the monasteries.

It is with this last activity that Cromwell's name will always be chiefly associated. He was the direct author of the great orgy of loot which follows thenceforward for the better part of a lifetime, and his motive in this move was personal gain. The whole of his life had been devoted to acquiring wealth, usually by the basest means, and that sufficiently accounts for all that he did in the matter of the religious houses.

He began by suppressing the smaller houses—that is, those whose incomes were less than what we should call to-day about five thousand pounds a year. These smaller houses accounted for barely a quarter of the monastic wealth of England. The whole thing was arranged after a fashion which testified highly to Cromwell's ability, for it was so worked that things should lead on from one step to another until all the monastic and conventual life of England was destroyed.

The first step was merely to take an inventory and to begin an examination into the alleged irregularities of certain houses; the next was to declare a policy of confiscation for the smaller houses, on the plea that they were generally badly managed and often corrupt. But while this was going on there was no hint of attack on monasticism as a religious principle or on the monastic wealth as a whole. The heads of the great houses acquiesced in the movement. Monks and nuns from the smaller houses were drafted into the larger houses, and Cromwell gave it to be understood that the money taken from the suppressed small houses would be used for pious purposes.

Then came the last step. No law was made compelling the surrender of the great houses, like the law that had been made to compel the surrender of the smaller ones. Some were seized on the plea that they had been treasonable, in others the Abbot was heavily bribed to surrender his house peacefully to the King, in others some charge of theft or other crime was trumped up against the ruling head of the establishment, till altogether, in one way or another, every single one of the great monastic houses of England was surrendered to the King and ceased to exist.

The wealth did not stay in the King's hands, of course. Cromwell himself made a very large fortune out of the pickings. He gave no less than thirteen monastic estates to his nephew (of whom more in a moment) and he gave land as benefactions right and left, as also did the King. Later on much of the Abbey lands thus confiscated were given away to favourites of the Court or, what was very common, were sold at half the price or less.

It is one of the commonest things for such of the so-called Reformation families as remain—that is, the English families whose wealth is founded on the loot of the Church in the sixteenth century—to boast that they paid for their land honestly, but when you look into the details you continually find that they got it for an average of ten years' rent—a sum which was about half the market prices of the estates.

Cromwell's motive in this gigantic economic revolution, which made about one-fifth of the upper-class surplus incomes of England change hands, was merely loot. But the ultimate effect, which he did not directly intend, was to create a strong vested interest against reconciliation with Rome. The looted land was sold and resold; as time passed families which had not been enriched married into those which had, and at last pretty well every landed family in England had been, as it were, "bribed" not to admit England's being made Catholic again.

Even when Mary Tudor, long after Cromwell's death, proposed reconciliation with the Papacy, the English upper classes refused to consider the idea unless the Pope would solemnly promise they could keep the stolen lands—which the Pope reluctantly did. Even so, it was their possession of the Abbey lands which determined all the position of the English gentry for a lifetime and made them determined to prevent the return of the Mass to England.

As an example of one of these families, let me return to Thomas Cromwell's own nephew, of whom I spoke. Cromwell's sister married a young man, the son of another ale-house keeper in Putney, called Williams-ap-Williams. She had a son, Henry, whom Thomas Cromwell took up and advanced, making him, before he died, entirely out of Church loot, one of the wealthiest men in England. The nephew dropped the name of Williams for the name of Cromwell, established his son as a great magnate, with his principal seat built out of the ruins of a stolen nunnery at Hinchingbrooke; and that son's grandson was the Oliver Cromwell of the next century.

Thomas Cromwell thus ruled England (becoming one of the richest men of the country in the process) right on till 1540. His power was, of course, very offensive to the old nobles, and even the new upstarts were jealous of him. But he feared nothing from them so long as he could manage the King.

What broke down his hold over the King was a ludicrously simple incident. He over-estimated his power and tried to make Henry, who had long ago put Anne Boleyn to death, and whose succeeding wife, Jane Seymour, had died, marry into one of the lesser German Protestant princes' families, that of the Duke of Cleves, on the lower Rhine.

Cromwell's foreign policy was not Protestant in any religious sense; he was during all his active life indifferent to religion altogether; but it paid him to tie Henry up with the Protestant princes of Germany if he could, so that there could be no going back upon the schism, and so that also his own vast fortune, built out of confiscated Church lands, could be secure.

When Anne of Cleves came over to be married, Henry was disgusted with her. Always impulsive and weak as he was, he fell into a furious temper with Cromwell for having let him in for such a botheration as this unsuitable marriage. Meanwhile the Howards, the heads of the older nobility and close connections by marriage of Henry's, were working ceaselessly against Cromwell's power, as was Henry's brother-in-law, Seymour, the uncle of the little boy who would be the King's heir.

What with Henry's raging bad temper at having been bamboozled into the Anne of Cleves marriage, what with his irritation in feeling that Cromwell acted as though he were supreme in the State, and what with the Howards and the Seymours pushing the King on, the determination was taken to get rid of Cromwell at last, and in the early summer of 1540, when he was a man of well over fifty and at the height of his power and wealth, he was suddenly arrested at the Council board.

He was condemned to death by attainder without trial and made the few days between the condemnation and his death both pitiable and memorable by the imploring letters which he wrote the King begging and even screaming for life. He ended one of them with the famous cry, "Mercy! Mercy! Mercy!" He fawned and cringed, using the most extraordinary phrases, comparing Henry to God and saying that the perfume of the royal hand would waft him to Heaven if he were allowed to kiss it again.

But it was all in vain: he was to die, and die he did on July 28, 1540.

Then on the scaffold a strange thing happened. Cromwell had the reputation of being perfectly indifferent to religion, an atheist concerned only with this world and therefore utterly without scruple. He had supported the anti-Catholic movement with all his might because it made his loot secure. Now that he was about to die he declared himself, to the astonishment of everybody, a firm adherent of the national and traditional faith. His sincerity has been doubted, but without sufficient grounds.

I think the matter is clear enough. He had been horribly afraid of death all his life—a trait, by the way, which you also find in his great-nephew, Oliver. He therefore would never contemplate death, and therefore also put religion out of his mind. But when he was face to face with death and had to deal with it somehow he admitted Catholic truth and confessed his acceptance of it. The phenomenon is not uncommon and is quite explicable by all that we know of the human mind.

Whether this last repentance saved him or not we cannot tell. But his work was accomplished before his head fell; he had effected the breach with Rome, and by his loot of the Church he had made possible all the further steps by which England was transformed to a Protestant from a Catholic country, at the same time giving the whole governing class of England a strong financial motive for never allowing the Mass to return to England if they could help it.

That class, which still has much of its old power, remains to this day the chief enemy of the Catholic Church.

SAINT THOMAS MORE

THE PORTRAIT of Saint Thomas More, in any serious dealing with the English Reformation, must differ in quality from any of the other portraits in this fashion: That it is the portrait of a medium through which we are enabled to understand what the English mind of that day was.

In other words, we do not, as in the case of Catherine of Aragon or Henry, Anne Boleyn, Cromwell, or any of the others, concern ourselves particularly with the external events of the man's life. They may be told briefly; they are easily summarized and they are universally known. He was born in the high and wealthy legal world of Catholic England, thirteen years before King Henry VIII. He inherited, and stepped naturally into, the greatest honours and legal position. He abandoned them all and died for the Faith.

There is no problem of a political nature attached to that famous name. There is no plot or intrigue. We have not to seek out and guess what was really at work in him by way of ambition or anything of that kind. What we can do, and what is of importance, is to understand what the man was interiorly, what kind of victory it was which he won, and how what he was, and the victory he won, explain the time.

The task is all the more necessary because, in a very subtle way but a very important one, the Saint Thomas More is badly misunderstood; and through misunderstanding him we misunderstand the nature of the English Reformation itself as well as the peculiar and individual greatness of this individual martyr.

What I may call the conventional portrait of the man, the one which both Catholics and Protestants accept (for he is quite as much admired in the other camp as in ours) is something as follows:

"While most of England was following the lead of King Henry and cutting itself off from the unity of the Church, and while the country as a whole was going Protestant, a few men among the laity stood out for the

55

old Catholic position. They would not listen to any talk of a breach with the Papacy, which they knew to be of Divine institution, and the very keystone of the Church. Therefore they boldly sacrificed themselves rather than give way to the new claims of the lay State or admit Henry to be the supreme head of the Church or accept Protestant doctrine or admit that Anne Boleyn was queen, or that her child Elizabeth could legitimately become queen after her. Of these very few laymen who so stood out, the most distinguished was a great lawyer, a man of good birth, who had early acquired a great position at the Bar, and had become Lord Chancellor of England. He was also a great scholar, and eminent throughout Europe. But he laid down his life in the cause of the Church as against Protestantism, and on that account has been canonized."

That, I say, is roughly the picture presented. Now the true picture tells us things far more profound and the character it presents is far more subtle, far more tempted, and far more an example of sanctity and martyrdom than so simple a summary would lead us to believe.

The external side of this conventional portrait is right enough. Thomas More *was* a great lawyer who had early achieved fame and fortune in his profession, had become Lord Chancellor of England, *was* eminent throughout Europe for his scholarship, a great international figure, and *was* put to death for refusing to deny a point of Catholic doctrine. What is wrong about it is the internal interpretation. Those who thus simplify the story, making it a plain scheme of black and white, do so either because they are insufficiently acquainted with the details of that career, or because the right emphasis is not laid in the right places by those from whom they have drawn their information. Further, the conventional portrait, which I have just sketched, implies a misunderstanding of the spirit abroad at the time of the English Reformation.

The whole point of the *true* story is twofold: 1. The great Martyr whom we venerate had all the intellectual and moral difficulties which attach to genius of his kind. 2. He acted alone. He was unsupported.

As to the first point: He had the temptations which beset the intellectual man, the sensitive scholar, the successful worldly figure. To these temptations he was in danger of yielding, and *had partly yielded*. He triumphed over them, and that in a fashion quite peculiar to himself. That is why he is so glorious, and that is why he is so great an example. Sir Thomas More was not simply a Catholic withstanding a movement towards Protestantism. Had he been that he would have been like almost any other Englishman of his time. He was not simply a man determined on defending

Catholic doctrine and boldly proclaiming it at all risks because it was his nature thus to challenge and to combat. Had he been of such a sort his victory over himself would have been far less than it was.

As to the second point: Let us note this all-important matter, which is the very core of his great sacrifice: he acted in complete isolation, and he laid down his life for one small strict point of Catholic doctrine only; and, what is more, a point of doctrine *on which he had himself long doubted.* He was not supported by the military spirit, the combative energy which delights in challenge and in counter affirmation. He was not supported by any sympathy for himself even among his nearest. He was not supported by the nature of his own mind, which had been hesitant and, even in essential matters, changeable. He gave himself up as a victim *in spite of* all those things which would make nine hundred and ninety-nine men out of a thousand deceive themselves that they might be doing right in yielding.

This is the heroic and almost unique quality in More.

To begin with let it clearly be understood that Saint Thomas More was a reformer. The whole of Europe was in turmoil between the old scholastic culture and the new passion for pagan antiquity which was making Greek scholarship so powerful an instrument of criticism against ancient ideas and habits in religion. The whole of Christendom was moved also by a spirit which caused the younger men especially, and more especially the more intelligent and emotional of the younger men, to denounce the corruptions of the time, the errors of legend, the exaggeration of certain practices and the doubtfulness or demonstrable falsity of many shrines and relics.

Sir Thomas More was just of the kind who would, according to the mere order of nature, have drifted from step to step, beginning with indignation against abuses, and ending with the full heretical position into which nearly all such men later fell.

He was indignant against the social order of his time as well as against the abuses of the Church. What is more, his indignation inspired him to wit, and to very high literary efforts; and men who discover such talents in themselves while they are still young nearly always fall into the temptation of becoming increasingly revolutionary as time proceeds. Sir Thomas More should, therefore, according to the order of nature, have become ultimately a violent opponent not only of the social order but of that Divine unity in the Church for which he laid down his life. All his character seemed to point that way.

Again, he began as a man of profound worldly ambition. He fully recognized his own talents, and he gloried in them. They had led him to the highest political position in the State. Such a temper should naturally have made him in the long run acquiesce in all official action.

Again, he was a man full of humour, and also full of domestic affection. He keenly felt how ridiculous a man looks in any isolated position, how absurd it is to be a "crank," and he felt still more keenly misunderstandings with any of his own household. Such a man should naturally shrink more than would another from any action, let alone the acceptation of death itself, in which he would suffer the public accusation of eccentricity and perverseness, and the reproaches of his own wife.

Lastly, there is this point about the isolation of this martyr. He could foresee no fruit following upon his great example. In fact, during all the four hundred years from his day to ours, no apparent political fruit has been borne by it.

He was absolutely alone. He had nothing within or without, nothing promised in the future, nothing inherited from the past, nothing in the traditions of his habits and life, to nerve him for what he did. And yet he did it.

In order to understand how extraordinary the case is, and what a marvellous example it is of resolution and vision combined, let us appreciate exactly what it was that the Blessed Thomas More defended at the cost of his life.

He died for the principle, that ultimately, in spiritual matters, the Pope was the Head of Christendom—a principle which all Christendom was debating, and had been debating for more than a hundred years, and on which all his lay world in England differed from him.

He did not die for the Real Presence, as did many another after him. He did not die, as many another might have done, out of loyalty to Queen Catherine. He did not die as a protest against a doctrine generally held heretical. Still less did he die rather than give up some old fixed habit of mind, attached to the ancient civilization of his country. He was not a man merely angry against change. On the contrary, he had been all for change. He did not die, even, at the end of a long public protest against the way in which things were drifting. He did not die for the Mass or for the sanctity of the clerical order. He died only for that one point of the Papal Supremacy, then universally doubted and one on which it was common-sense to compromise.

To us to-day it seems an obvious thing to say, "Oh, but the Papal Supremacy is the very test of Catholicism!"

So Sir Thomas More himself saw; but so did *not* see the mass of his contemporaries, and so had he himself *not* seen a very short time before.

When Henry VIII had himself been working against the Lutherans in favour of the Papal office, and saying that the Papacy was of Divine institution, Sir Thomas More had been of the opinion that it was *not* so. He had decided, from his reading up to that point, that the Papacy was no more than an historical development, bound up no doubt with the structure of the Church, but of human origin, as is the most of ecclesiastical organization. A hundred years before he would have been essentially by temperament one of those naturally supporting the authority of the great Councils and thinking them superior to Rome. Yet it was for that very point, which he had himself doubted, that he consented to die.

Observe the circumstances of that death, and see how strange they were compared with what might be called, with due respect, the general run of martyrdoms.

The King had determined to get his true marriage declared null, to make Anne Boleyn his queen, and to make Anne Boleyn's child his heir. Sir Thomas More did not protest when he saw that the royal policy was drifting more and more away from unity with the Holy See; he resigned his office, but he did so without explanation. If another should take his place who had not these scruples, he would raise no voice against the newcomer.

When the royal supremacy was declared in its final and most conclusive form, in November of 1534, and the Pope was repudiated (though the Mass and everything else went on as usual) he remained what was called, in the language of the day, a loyal subject to his "natural Lord," King Henry.

He did not challenge; he remained silent, so far as official action went, although, of course, his private conviction was known.

Even when the Oath of Supremacy was administered he was prepared to accept the marriage of Henry with Anne, and to admit that their child should inherit the throne, through the disinheritance of the true heiress, the Princess Mary.

When the document was put before him for his acceptance, to be sworn to in the presence of Cranmer at Lambeth in the Archbishop's palace, he made no protest against it as a whole. All he said was that *there was a point in the Preamble which he could not accept.* He held out over a detail—or what seemed to contemporaries a detail. "One poor scruple." He said that the Preamble implied something he could not in conscience accept.

They did not want to sacrifice him. They bade him think it over; and he walked up and down in the gardens of Lambeth palace thinking it over, as they thought, but he was not likely to think himself into another state of mind. He stood firm, on that one small point: that the phraseology of one small part of a law which, in everything else, he accepted, was at issue with orthodoxy. For that he was imprisoned, for that, many months after, he willingly accepted death.

When they went through the form of trial in the last days before his sacrifice, it is remarkable to observe how silent he still remained, how wholly upon the defensive, still asking his opponents to prove their case, and keeping back in reserve all that he might have said. Until sentence was delivered no man could have proved out of his own mouth what that doctrine was for which none the less he was ready to lay down his life. Only when sentence had been passed did he speak at last, fully, and tell them precisely what his position was.

To his own family as a whole probably, to his wife certainly, to nearly all his friends and to the mass of Englishmen of his time, his position was not heroic but absurd. The King was already head of everything in England, and had been for generations past. He nominated to the Bishoprics and great Abbeys; his was the supreme court of appeal in nearly everything that mattered, and even though there was in this last declaration of full supremacy something novel, yet a quarrel between King and Pope was something with which Englishmen had been familiar over and over again for centuries. It would heal quickly, no doubt, as the others had done and at any rate such political broils were nothing to sacrifice one's fortune for, let alone one's life. If indeed someone must stand out and be dramatic in the matter, and overdo the histrionics in the now quite out of date Thomas-á-Becket fashion, why, let it be a priest at least, and best of all some great prelate. No doubt men could understand Bishop Fisher: but why Thomas More?

He was, I repeat, utterly alone. He had no support from without.

And what support had he from within? That terrible question we cannot answer with certitude, but we can, I think, with probability. I think he had very little support from within. His was not only a sceptical mind, as has been the mind of more than one who has none the less suffered death for truth held by faith and not by experience: it was also a mind which had long practice of seeing both sides of any question aid thinking anything could be argued; on that particular point of the Papacy he had himself argued sincerely enough upon the wrong side. I suggest that the Martyr in his last moments had all the intellectual frailty of the intellectuals, and that at the end his scepticism was still working; but his glorious resolution stood—and that is the kernel of the affair. He had what is called "Heroic Faith."

Could he return to earth to-day he would note with that irony of which he was a master that his sacrifice would seem to have been in vain. Whether it were so or not only a distant future can tell. But this much is certain, that of all those, and they were many, who bore witness in the five generations it took to root out their age-long religion from among the English, his would seem to have been the most complete passion; for he had nothing whatever to uphold him except resolve.

POPE CLEMENT THE SEVENTH

CLEMENT VII was the Pope of King Henry VIII's divorce. He was reigning over the whole space of that affair, being appointed before the King of England had any intention of getting rid of his wife, and dying after the English schism had been virtually completed and within a very short time of its final and formal completion by the Act of Supremacy. For Henry's idea of getting rid of his legitimate wife, Catherine of Aragon (which idea as we have seen was probably more Anne Boleyn's than his own), cannot have arisen, at the very earliest, before 1525. The first (not absolutely certain) documentary allusion to it is in 1526, and overt action only begins in 1527. Now Clement VII was elected to the Papal throne in 1523.

Again, the last political acts by which the separation of England from the unity of the Catholic Church was made certain filled the years 1533–34. In 1533 you get the divorce pronounced by Cranmer in spite of the Papal prohibition, the marriage with Anne Boleyn acknowledged and her crowning as Queen, the birth of Elizabeth and the declaration by law of her legitimacy (though she was illegitimate in the eyes of all Europe and of course in those of ecclesiastical authority); while in the year 1534 you get all the acts one after another which culminated in the complete separation of England from Rome. That was already accomplished before the summer of 1534, and the seal was set upon the whole process by the full Act of Supremacy in the first days of November of that year: for it was the custom of any English Parliament that might be summoned to meet on or just after All Souls' Day. Clement died only six weeks earlier, at the end of September in that same year.

He is therefore the man in supreme authority during all the period of the divorce and of the schism.

Now the prime historical question which his reign arouses is this. Could the position have been saved? Could the Pope, by the exercise of certain virtues or certain intellectual qualities in a fashion different from that which he actually showed, have prevented the loss of England to the unity of the Faith? It is a question of the very first importance to the whole history of Europe for, as I am never tired of repeating, if England had not gone Christendom would still be united and all Europe would be Catholic to-day.

The answer to this question is not, I think, doubtful. Though Clement was guilty of great weakness and of tortuous policy, though he often sacrificed the spiritual to the temporal, yet he cannot be made responsible for the disaster. Nothing could have prevented the schism save the Pope's pronouncement in favour of a divorce, and that the Pope could not do without flying in the face of Christian law, of which he was the supreme guardian by the nature of his office.

In order to appreciate the truth of this let us begin by appreciating who and what Pope Clement was. He was the son of Julian de Medici, who in his turn was the brother of the famous Lorenzo de Medici, that great despot of Florence generally called Lorenzo the Magnificent—not only one of the wealthiest and one of the most powerful Princes of the Renaissance, but also one of the most striking of the many striking characters of that time.

The Medicis were a family which had grown enormously rich in commerce amid a commercial community, their fortunes being undoubtedly helped by many an evil practice and particularly by usury and oppression. They had become so wealthy that they ranked with reigning sovereigns; John, the second son of Lorenzo, became, through the influence of the Medicean name and its vast financial interests as also through his own striking character and the excellent training he had had, an obvious candidate for the Papacy, as the Papacy then was, unfortunately, with its great worldly interests and overlaid by the idea men had of it (including the Popes themselves) that it was not only the supreme head of the Church but an Italian Principate. It was this John de Medici, reigning as Leo X, who was Pope when the great outbreak in Germany took place. He and his advisers, as we know, misunderstood it; and so the Lutheran movement grew under his reign. His Court was splendid, his patronage of the arts glorious and fruitful, he himself was of good life and a scholar, but all that side of his character—eminently fitted for the general and worldly duties of his supreme office—was of worldly influence only; worldly he was and worldly wealth and interests did he represent. He kept at his side, to help him manage the political side of the Church, this cousin of his—Julius, the son of his father's brother Julian. Julius de Medici was made Cardinal and was the right-hand man of his cousin Leo X during the reign. After the brief interval of that very fine reforming character Adrian VI (who, if he had lived, might well have reversed the current and reunited Europe), Julius de Medici was elected at the age of forty-five under the title of Clement VII.

He was a man of excellent morals, very great erudition, good manners, perfect refinement, if anything rather too much delicacy of mind and of taste, a splendid patron of the arts and a sure judge of excellence in them. He was also a remarkably hard worker, taking the tremendous duties of his office most seriously. Moreover he was as intelligent as any man in Europe. What he lacked was simplicity, also strength of initiative and power of direction. He lacked both those qualities which make for strong command through what may be called the "squareness" of a character, and those which make for successful command through the moral simplicity of a character. In the face of a difficult and involved position his policy became a tangle of secret and involved intrigues, and he had that fatal symptom of weakness which takes the form of always playing for time. There are, obviously, occasions when playing for time is wise, but Clement VII was one of those men who always play for time, and when they find a decision difficult, say to themselves that with sufficient delay anything may turn up in their favour, and who therefore create delay for its own sake. All his method, from the first mention of the desire for divorce expressed by the English Court up to the very last still hesitating and half tentative declarations against the actions of the English government, consisted in dependence on delay. For seven years he played delay as his only card.

Nevertheless for all his weakness and for all his errors, he could not, I repeat, have prevented the disaster. Or at least, he could only have prevented it at the price of disloyalty to the prestige and power and supernatural claims of the Papacy which it was his first duty to protect. Had he hastened things and pronounced against Henry in as brief a time as could, with decency and the observation of forms, have been managed, the schism would still have taken place; because those who were managing the impulsive, sensual and therefore weak will of the English King were determined to have the divorce, or, if they could not get it, to break with the Head of Christendom and have it pronounced upon the local authority of their own servant, the Primate of England. They had behind them not only the will of Anne Boleyn and later the powerful brain and capacity for rule of Cromwell, but the driving power of universal greed in the wealthier classes, who were straining at the leash to be let loose upon the property of the Church.

I take it that the earliest date on which Clement might have definitely pronounced for or against Henry's claim was late in 1530, or more probably early in 1531. In practice, perhaps, considering all the obstacles of forms, appeals and the rest, it might have been impossible before 1532. At any such stage it would have been too late. To have granted the divorce against justice and ecclesiastical law would have ruined the already shaken Papal office, quite apart from the fact that Catherine belonged to the most powerful ruling family of Europe. But it is equally true—and that is what people miss—that if Clement had been a more straightforward man and had pronounced in favour of the Queen at the earlier date and against Henry, it would have been already too late to save England. Henry was already thoroughly and openly in the hands of Anne Boleyn and already privately in the hands of Thomas Cromwell with the whole of the English territorial class ready, under the protection of Anne and Cromwell, to spring upon the revenues of religion.

It has been the general fashion for your official anti-Catholic historian, both of the English and German Protestant variety and of the French and Italian anti-clerical variety, to ascribe Clement's reluctance to pronounce in favour of the divorce to the fear and pressure of the great Emperor Charles V, Queen Catherine's nephew and the head of her family. Too many Catholics have been affected by the general trend of the written history around them, and have half assented to this idea. It is a false judgment.

Clement's mere political intentions during all his reign were obvious enough, and even necessary. His policy was certainly not merely to yield to the powerful Emperor. It was rather to play the Emperor's power against that of the French King (with whom was in alliance during all the latter part of the business the government of Henry of England) and thus be independent of both.

It is true that he was reconciled with Charles V, after having been treated as a virtual prisoner by the irregular troops of that Emperor. It is true that after long double negotiations, and the secret support of Charles' rivals, he came to an open agreement and crowned Charles at Bologna in 1530. It is true that of the various great political forces pulling the Papacy various ways the force of Charles V was at the critical moment (1532) the greatest; but it is *not* true that it decided the issue. What decided the issue was the necessity that any Pope would have been under—strong or weak—straightforward or intriguing—to decide upon the merits of the case.

Clement went to the extreme limits of concession to Henry VIII, or rather to those who ran Henry VIII. He went beyond the limits of due and rightful concession. The weakest and most blamable of all his acts was a secret promise that he would not recall the case to Rome but let it be concluded in Henry's kingdom and under Henry's eye. It is true that this promise was conditional, that Clement left himself a loophole of which he could take advantage, and of which he did take advantage when Catherine lodged her appeal. Still, it was intended to deceive and cause delay and was an act the more reprehensible on that account.

Yet even with all such concessions, with all his hesitation and chance phrases which seemed to give Henry hope of succeeding, the central fact remained, Catherine had solemnly denied the consummation of the original marriage; she was a woman of high character, she swore she had never been the real wife of Henry's brother who had died as a boy, and Henry never contradicted her.

Proof sufficient to overset that solemn declaration was lacking; there was no sufficient ground upon which to quash the marriage of Catherine with Henry and declare it null, *unless* Clement had been willing to admit that he was not the supreme judge in a moral case, that is, unless he had been willing to stultify all the claims and position of the Papacy. He had himself said in his despair and anxiety that it would be a good thing if the Queen of England were in her grave. He had allowed all manner of suggestions for outflanking the difficulty. He had even considered Catherine's voluntary renunciation—and of course everything would have been made easy if Catherine had consented no longer to press her solemn declaration or to insist upon her appeal. But, with Catherine making that appeal and taking the position she did, Clement had no choice but to act as he acted, even at the risk of losing England and perhaps, so delicate was the situation, France the ally of England, as well.

Those who have blamed him most have failed to emphasize his chief grounds for hesitancy and delay, grounds which would have affected even the strongest character. All Christendom appeared to be breaking up. And though England was but a comparatively small and weak power compared with France or the Empire, what side she would take in the universal religious struggle was bound to make all the difference; and a Pope must needs think twice or three times before he determined—however great the moral necessity—to risk the loss of England.

We may sum up the situation by saying that if a stronger and more direct mind had been at work in the successor of St. Peter the English schism would have arrived with less loss of honour and moral authority to Rome. But we must add that much as Clement's weakness and shuffling must be regretted, he never passed the boundary beyond which there is abdication or denial of authority. He never compromised the fundamentals of the Papal power and of its awful claim to moral supremacy among men.

There is something supernatural in all this. We always have to be careful in history not to exaggerate evidence of the supernatural, nor to ascribe to supernatural causes what may legitimately be ascribed to natural ones, but here there seems to be evidence of supernatural guidance. Just one step too far at one moment in Papal history would have compromised the Papacy in the eyes of posterity and have given solid argument against its claims. That moment fell in the reign of Clement VII. And in that moment the Papacy did not fail, even though the Pope had sailed so very near the wind. Clement just might, at the most critical moment when he was being hardest pressed, bullied, not knowing what to do between the great contending forces of which he was the victim, he just might, I say, have overstepped the limit. He might, for instance, have issued a Bull in which he declared the original Papal power of dispensation for marriage with a sister-in-law to be void. He might have got out of his difficulties by allowing the verdict of the universities to be, not advisory to the Holy See, but upon an equality with it. He might have taken any one of half a dozen steps, each of which would have been, for the first time, an admission by a Pope that the Papacy was not what it was. And, by a sufficient margin, Clement happily was preserved from so fatal an excess of weakness.

He was preserved from it by that Divine safeguarding of the Church which never fails; but he was also preserved from it by that element in him which, for all his faults, remained strong: a recognition of what was essential to his office.

THOMAS CRANMER

THOMAS CRANMER in the gallery of the English Reformation is the counterpart to Thomas Cromwell.

Between them they might be called the authors of the tragedy; but in very different fashions. Cromwell was the author in the sense of the man who creates; Cranmer was never more than an agent though a willing agent—even in his heart of hearts an enthusiastic agent: a man who hated the Catholic Church and the Sacraments and in especial the Sacrament of the Altar and the Mass; whereas Cromwell was indifferent to religion, or rather let his sense of religion sink out of his consciousness, till it reappeared in his last moments upon the scaffold—in the presence of the death which he so greatly dreaded.

Cromwell, of all those who came across Henry VIII as one of his officials, was the one who most mastered the King and who could best boast that the policy of the country was entirely in his hands. Cranmer, of all those who came into official contact with Henry, was the most completely subservient and least able to impose himself.

But the way in which Cranmer was the counterpart of Cromwell in the story of the movement was most noticeable in one particular character. Cromwell, who should by rights be regarded as the chief figure of the time, has not received the full attention he should from popular historians or from the public: Cranmer has.

Cranmer, who was essentially a subsidiary figure, has received the fullest attention. Until quite recently any average English Protestant you might speak to of any degree of instruction—high or low, rich or poor—could have told you the central facts about Cranmer; how he was the great Archbishop of Canterbury who helped Henry to break with Rome, how he had made the Liturgy of the new Protestant service, and especially how he had been martyred under Queen Mary, being burnt alive after a moment's weakness of which he gloriously repented and which he expiated by his willing and terrible sacrifice. Especially was one story remembered as one of the principal and popularly traditional things in English history, how he thrust into the fire when he was being burnt the hand which had signed the recantations, saying, "This was the hand that did it!"

But if you were to ask the same men what they knew of Cromwell, most of them would say that they had only heard of one Cromwell called Oliver, and those who had heard of Thomas Cromwell might vaguely remember that he had something to do with putting down the monasteries.

Cromwell, by the scale of his intelligence, his understanding of national and international affairs, his strength of will, tenacity of purpose, grasp of detail—all that marks a great statesman—was almost on the level of Bismarck or Richelieu. His extreme vileness and baseness, his brutality and gross cowardice at the end does not affect this judgment as to his capacity, which he put to such abominable uses.

But Cranmer showed little intelligence or foresight, was devoid of initiative, accepted through fear the various tasks thrust upon him, was always subservient, and by nature hypocritical and wavering. He did not want to be Chaplain to Anne Boleyn in particular, though no doubt he was glad of the income: he did not want to plead for Henry VIII at Rome: he certainly did not want to be made Archbishop; he took but a petty part in the spoiling of the Church and allowed his own diocese to be spoiled unmercifully.

After being the mere servant of Henry and ready to belie any conviction of his own at Henry's orders he became the servant of the tyrant Somerset after Henry's death, then the servant of the man who supplanted that tyrant, then it was he who pitifully attempted to save his life under Mary by the most abject denials and repudiation of all that he really had at heart.

There was one quality indeed about Cranmer which many have mistaken for greatness; and it is the one which we must linger upon, because error in this matter is so common, not only in his case but in a hundred others.

Cranmer had great artistic power. He could frame a sentence of rhythmical and exquisitely beautiful English as no man has been able to do before or since. It is to him that the Anglican Church owes those prayers, "The English Prayerbook", the diction and language of which have given it its strong hold upon the national mind. The Litany of the English Church is his—a wonderful document as far as artistry is concerned; presumably most of the Collects, the translation of the Prefaces of the Mass incorporated into the English service, and many other Catholic prayers similarly incorporated.

His unique talent was not recognized in his lifetime; its effect upon men's minds came much later; the strong affection which the average Englishman feels for the Book of Common Prayer and its fine phrases dates, not from Cranmer's century but from the next. It is often the case with great artists in prose and verse; they need time to manifest their gifts and these are not apparent until long after they are dead.

Cranmer having such supreme talent, in this one line of writing exquisite prose, a modern habit of mind would make us confuse such talent with real greatness. And it is at this point that I beg the reader to pause and consider how false such an attitude is.

Great artistic talent in any direction, as of a poet or a prose writer or a painter or a sculptor or anything else, is hardly inherent to the man; it comes and goes; it is often possessed only for a short phase in his life; it hardly ever colours his character as a whole and has nothing to do with the moral and intellectual stuff of the mind and soul—by which alone men's intrinsic greatness can be measured. Many great artists, perhaps most great artists, have been poor fellows indeed, whom to know was to despise.

So it was with Cranmer, and it is further to be remarked that he was one of those artists who can only work in a very limited frame. He wrote great masses of stuff both in Latin and English, plenty of letters, disputations, reports and the rest, most of them turgid and none of them remarkable. He only produced this astonishing prose when he sat down to do it with great care, thinking about every word and concentrating upon the narrow task before him. And, as is always the case with this kind of talent, he only excelled in short passages. With all this it must be remembered that Cranmer stands at the origin of great English prose. He was not only the highest master of it but he was also the chief originator of it. By that alone has he any claims to fame.

What the man was himself a brief recital of his life suffices to show. He was the younger son of a small gentleman, that is a small squire of land, in the English Midlands; he was brought up therefore to country sports, was always a very good rider and a good shot with the bow, which was odd because he had bad sight and in reading or writing he had to keep his face close to the paper and peer at his work.

He was destined for the Church simply by way of providing an income for him, as was the custom with the younger sons of his class. He was made a member of a very small insignificant foundation, Jesus College, in what was then the reduced university of Cambridge. He lived there for years, until he was nearly forty (he was about two years older than Henry VIII but somewhat younger than Cromwell) leading the obscure life of a scholar with a certain amount of local reputation as an examiner in theology.

He had had, before taking Holy Orders, an adventure (which seems not to have been very reputable but which ended in marriage) with a servant at an inn in Cambridge, and after her early death was taken back again into the fellowship of his College.

The violent movement, which had begun as criticism partly scholarly and partly theological of clerical corruption and which soon turned into revolt against the Church, laid hold of a small but very active minority in Cambridge while he was passing there through early manhood to middle age. But though he certainly sympathized with all attacks upon Catholicism—for he had begun to hate the religion of his upbringing—yet he was too timid to give any active expression to his feelings, for all the official world of England was strongly orthodox and even after the break with Rome, Henry, as we know, insisted upon the teaching of full Catholic doctrine in everything but the Papacy, and on the Mass, and the Sacraments, and everything else in the general life of a Catholic people.

Cranmer was at Cambridge when Erasmus was beginning his work there; but he seems not even to have met Erasmus; he was there when Barnes preached his famous revolutionary sermon, he was there when all the small group of enthusiastic religious revolutionaries were running their risks—but he himself ran no risk at all.

What brought him into prominence was the fact that two men in whom Henry placed great reliance, Gardiner—a man of great capacity whom Wolsey had made important and who was Secretary of State to Henry—and Fox, Gardiner's right-hand man, recommended him to the King. They were both Cambridge men and thus knew of Cranmer; they were certainly acquainted with the fact that he could write and with his local reputation for reading in theology and power to argue theological points.

When, therefore, Cranmer, in a private conversation, supported the idea of appealing to the universities of Europe against the Pope (an idea which he did not originate—it had already been discussed for two years) Henry sent for him and bade him draw up a brief or argument in favour of his divorce. At the same time Cranmer was put to live in the Boleyns' household, but it seems probable, from a phrase of Cardinal Pole's, that he already had some connection with the Boleyns before then.

At any rate he becomes Anne Boleyn's Chaplain and is sent to Rome to plead the cause of the divorce before the Holy See; and then, when it became clear that Anne would never get rid of her legitimate rival, Queen Catherine, by Papal decision, and that she must rely upon an English Prelate of Henry's to pronounce the divorce, Cranmer—insignificant though he was—became her obvious candidate for the Primacy of England, that is the Archiepiscopal See of Canterbury.

Now at that moment anything that Anne Boleyn wanted to happen in England, did happen.

The aged and saintly Archbishop, Wareham, conveniently died in the year 1532, and Cranmer, having been hurriedly sent for from Italy, was made Archbishop. He was made Archbishop as a Catholic, in full communion with Rome and by leave of Rome, and took the oath of allegiance to the Pope; but he was put up to make a private declaration that he would perjure himself if necessity arose, since he did not regard his oath to the Pope as binding against the interest of the King. This of course was kept secret.

Cranmer then proceeded, at the orders of the King, to pronounce Henry's marriage with Catherine null; he was further ordered to crown Anne Boleyn as Queen; when her child Elizabeth was born he baptized her and stood godfather to her. Later, when Henry got tired of Anne Boleyn, Cranmer speedily turned against this woman to whom he owed all his promotion and position and in whose household he had been nourished; wormed out of her by feigned friendship some sort of admission of guilt, and betrayed her to Henry. His miserable weakness and subservience was thus guilty of her blood.

After that he did his best to help Cromwell secretly in the undermining of Catholicism in the country. He was particularly instrumental in deceiving the King over the new English translation of the Bible, which the King was assured was orthodox though the most essential words had been mistranslated so as to give Scripture, and particularly the New Testament, a Protestant sense. But he abandoned Cromwell just as he had abandoned Anne Boleyn, cringing to Henry when Cromwell fell into disfavour.

With Henry's later young wife, Catherine Howard, he played exactly the same trick he had played with Anne Boleyn. Catherine Howard represented the strongly Catholic faction, and it was Cranmer who gathered the denunciations against her, who wormed out a confession by feigned friendship and promises of forgiveness exactly as he had done in the case of Anne Boleyn; and he was guilty of Catherine Howard's blood as he had been guilty of Anne's.

So long as Henry lived he dared not say anything openly against the Catholic Church. He continued to say Mass with all due pomp and ceremony, much as lie had come to loathe the Holy Sacrifice and the Blessed Sacrament. He sent away the German wife whom he had secretly married because Henry would not have a married clergy; up to the very day of the King's death he played the part of orthodox Archbishop—Catholic in all save the schism with Rome.

The moment Henry was dead the gang who began to loot the Church still further and to try and impose Protestantism upon England under Somerset, the Protector of the young child upon the throne, found in Cranmer a willing helper. As I have said, when, within that gang, one tyrant proposed to oust another, he always followed the winning side.

During those six years which saw the first attempted extirpation of the Mass, and the rebellions of the people all over the place in defence of their religion, Cranmer was active in defending the tyranny and framing the new Protestant English service which was to replace the Immemorial Sacrifice. His name comes first in the list of those who proposed to make Lady Jane Grey Queen in order to keep out the legitimate heiress Mary; then when Mary was triumphantly brought into power on a wave of popular enthusiasm for her and for the Church, he makes abject apology in order to save his life.

But at that moment he was stung into the single action—the only one in his career—which shows but slight and hesitating courage. He strongly denied in private that he had ever said Mass at the Queen's orders. Men, knowing his wretched character, had taken it for granted that he would veer round once again; the report annoyed him and he therefore wrote this private protest. But he had not the courage to publish it; it was published in spite of him. He was thrown into prison, tried for heresy, convicted and deposed.

During his trial he shifted and wriggled perpetually, trying as best he could to get out of the position into which his flagrant recent acts had led him—for he had not only worked with all his might to destroy the Mass in England but had actually drawn up a code of laws by which men should be punished with death for accepting the Sacrament of the Altar.

Then, when he had been degraded from his episcopal office and function and condemned, he saw too late that they might really intend to put him to death, though hitherto to execute an Archbishop for heresy was a thing unheard of. He therefore made one recantation after another in the hope of saving his life.

These recantations became stronger and stronger as he went along, until at last he wrote out and published one of great length, in which he stretched to the utmost his professions of remorse and penitence. He threw himself upon the Divine Mercy, declared he was not worthy to live, said he deserved his fate, especially as he had led so many into error; and compared himself to the penitent thief on the cross, declaring that he could rely upon nothing but the infinite charity of Christ for such a case as his.

Up to the last moment he did not know whether these protestations of his had been effectual or not in deceiving the authorities. On the day fixed for the execution he was taken to St. Mary's Church in Oxford for his recantation to be made as public as possible and for a sermon to be preached upon it. The rule was, of course, that on such public recantation the prisoner for heresy was pardoned, and Cranmer had his recantation all ready to read. But while he sat there listening to the sermon preached about him, there came a phrase in that sermon which suddenly destroyed his hopes. The preacher had been told by the Government to announce their decision that they could not pardon Cranmer after all.

He then did a dramatic thing. He went up to read his recantation, but at the most critical point in it suddenly declared that all he had said in favour of the Church and against his former errors was insincere, and had merely been said in order to save his life. Now that he had to die anyhow he would confess that he was utterly opposed to the Catholic system and the Papacy and all the rest of it.

There was a great hubbub in the church, in the midst of which the little old man, still very vigorous though grown bald and nearly blind (he was not far from seventy years of age), ran through the rain with the congregation and the street mob at his heels, came out by the North Gate of the city and was clasped to the stake, which stood in front of Balliol College. As the smoke rose about him he was seen to put out his right hand, as he had said he would, putting it first into the fire as expiation for having signed his recantations.*

There is an historical and moral point of some importance connected with Cranmer's death. Had the authorities a right to act as they did? The answer would seem to be that technically they had such a right but that by custom and equity they had not. A heretic having once been condemned for obstinate heresy and handed over to the secular arm was from that moment subject to execution. But it had nearly always and everywhere been admitted in practice that if, even after the sentence, he recanted, he was to be saved. There were even cases in which a man actually recanting after

---

*The story has been queried because it was supposed to repose upon nothing but the word of Foxe, who is quite unreliable. But it is corroborated by contemporary testimony.

the fire had been lighted and obviously acting only under the influence of extreme suffering was released.

Therefore it may fairly be urged that Cranmer had by his abject and re-peated recantations earned the right to live at least, and that in putting him to death the Government was breaking an implied contract. On the other hand they could plead that the man's crimes had been so enormous and his position so especial that no reprieve for him could be possible.

To me personally the plea has always seemed insufficient. It seems to me unjust to have accepted these numerous recantations and to have obviously favoured their repetition and increasing emphasis, if they had not intended to spare him.

STEPHEN GARDINER

THE FIGURE of Stephen Gardiner is not among the very great figures of the English Reformation, or at any rate not quite in the first flight. On this account it has been in great part neglected, and quite unduly neglected, because although he did not mould events nor decide the general course of the movement, there is one reason for which all those who desire to understand the great disaster should make themselves well acquainted with this man. This reason is that he was the typical Englishman of the day.

If you follow the fortunes of Stephen Gardiner's soul, the fluctuation of his opinion, his utter devotion to national feeling, his original error on this account, his gradual awakening to the peril in which religion lay—his whole career, especially on its spiritual internal side—then you understand the England of the time.

Henry the King, impulsive and very vain, was certainly not a typical Englishman. Even Mary Tudor, with her half Spanish blood and her isolated mind, could not be called typical of the country; Cranmer was not, for he was too much of an artist and much too much of a time-server and a coward to be typical of any ordinary healthy normal citizen of any time or place. Elizabeth was still less typical of England, for both by her talents and by her diseases of body and soul she was an abnormality.

But Gardiner is the true Englishman of the time in body and mind and everything else. And that is his importance; understanding him, you understand the English Reformation, or rather you understand the kind of average citizen upon whom the catastrophe fell. It is, therefore, a great loss to history that even highly educated men have heard so little of him. For a hundred men who have heard of Henry, for fifty who have heard of Cranmer, perhaps one could tell you who Stephen Gardiner was.

Stephen Gardiner was born of that solid middle-class parentage which provided so many officials for the Tudor dynasty, especially those clerical officials who were its chief supports. We are not quite fixed on the date of his birth, but it came somewhere latish in the 1480's so that he was a little older than King Henry and some five to ten years younger than Saint Thomas More, the Lord Chancellor.

He went through the usual course of those middle-class lads who were destined for the Church—a career which in those days led to the highest political positions in men of temporal ability. He took his Doctorate of Law at Cambridge, and then became Wolsey's secretary. He was a man of about forty before he appeared in any very considerable political capacity, but by that time he was the regular Tudor civil servant of the day. He was a good ecclesiastic, but certainly at that time was putting his political office at least upon an equality with, and probably above his ecclesiastical. So far the man is simply one of a number of others, one of the regular Tudor official lot rewarded with various ecclesiastical preferments by the Kings whom they served.

He was a big strong man, with a square-jawed, heavy face, enlivened, however, by quick, large and brilliant dark eyes. He was fairly learned; he was a very able controversialist; he was a good speaker and a man full of health and energy.

The divorce business broke out just when he was established in this important official career, and the Government at once used him for their purpose. He had come from Wolsey's household (he had been, as I have said, Wolsey's secretary) and when Wolsey fell he became secretary to Henry; which meant, of course, that all important official documents passed through his hands, and that his judgment was in most things taken and considered. Into the affair of the divorce he threw himself heartily, acting wholly and simply as the servant of his sovereign. Of the bullying to which the unfortunate Pope was subjected the most extravagant and violent passages came from Gardiner himself. It was he at Rome who most directly threatened Clement with the danger of schism if he would not grant the divorce. He was wrapped up in the affair altogether without hesitation and without compromise, and the Court regarded him as so much their principal agent (and likely to be their most successful one in the business) that he was given the great Bishopric of Winchester as early as 1531, that is, long before the great business was decided and while it was in full swing.

The Bishop of Winchester in those days was one of the richest men in the kingdom; the office carried with it great political power as well. It had been the chief standby of Wolsey himself, and Gardiner, on obtaining it, became a very great man in English social and political life by mere rank, apart from what his talents and services had already proved him to be.

But here we may note a curious point. When it came to the danger of schism Gardiner had about him a touch of hesitation. It was only a touch, but it is significant of what was to come. He was still whole-heartedly in favour of that absolute kingly government and of that strong national feeling which went with it; he was still as much opposed as ever to the political Papal claims over temporal sovereigns, and especially over his own sovereign; and when the decision had to be taken he was ready to accept the supremacy of Henry over the Church of England, and even to defend it, as we shall see.

I pointed out in the case of Saint Thomas More, that to be so farsighted as to discern what the schism would ultimately mean was granted to very few. The average Englishman was with the King against the Pope in that particular quarrel—hoping vaguely perhaps that it would soon be patched up as so many others had been, but not connecting it in any way with doctrine. Therefore Gardiner, in every sense the average Englishman, followed the same road.

Yet he did show a slight hesitation when the exact formula by which the King's supremacy should be first hinted at was introduced into the debates of the clergy. It should always be remembered in this connection that the Royal Supremacy was not, in the first steps towards it, represented as schismatical; the full schism was only arrived at by degrees and after a series of steps, each of which, save the last, might be twisted or argued into orthodoxy.

Some have said that this hesitation of Gardiner's, slight as it was, caused him to be passed over when Wareham died and thus made him miss the Primacy, the Archbishopric of Canterbury; but this is a false judgment. Not Gardiner but Cranmer was marked out to be the next Archbishop because he was Anne Boleyn's man, her Chaplain, and because he was crapulous and would do anything he was told, as the future was to show. Those who think that there was any chance for Gardiner, misunderstand the position altogether, and particularly misunderstand the fact that it was Anne and not Henry who was running the whole affair.

Anyhow, Stephen Gardiner remained very prominent, the great Bishop of Winchester, full of wealth and power. He accepted the Supremacy; what is more, a year after the full schism had appeared—that is, in 1535—he engaged his responsibility up to the hilt by writing a tract in favour of a schismatic policy, the famous tract *De Vera Obedientia* ("Concerning True Obedience").

There is a characteristic letter of his to Bucer, the Continental Reformer, in which he gives us an example of the excellence of the Royal Supremacy compared with the Papal Supremacy on account of the better discipline it enforced throughout the Church in England. The King, he says, can strictly enforce the observation of celibacy, for instance, and can sharply correct the manners of his own clergy; while the Pope, under the circumstances of the time, where the Churches had become so largely national, was lacking in effective power.

In a word, Gardiner, in spite of that first half hesitation, was then (1534) whole-heartedly for Henry's position, for the Royal Supremacy in things spiritual as well as temporal and therefore, in practice, for the schism. And so he remained for years. He was a man of over sixty before he learnt the lesson, which all ultimately learnt, that there can be no Catholicism without the Pope.

To the modern mind that, of course, is a truism; indeed, to-day with so many people outside the Church apeing Catholicism and so many more interesting themselves in this or that aspect of Catholicism, it is a matter of course that the ultimate test of Catholicism is the acceptation of the Pope's authority. But we must always remember in reading of this period of the English Reformation this main point a neglect of which makes it incomprehensible: that the Papal claims were debated and had been debated for generations within the Catholic Church itself before the break-up of Christendom in the great disaster of the sixteenth century.

What with the political entanglements of temporal power, the Pope's political action as a mere Italian Prince, the very large sums taken by the Papacy in direct taxation from all countries, and the worldly character of too many Popes of the day—some of them an open scandal—it needed the experience of disunion to prove the necessity of union, and to prove in especial that the test of unity was obedience to the See of Peter.

When Bayard made his famous remark, "One can be a good Catholic without the Pope," he was saying what millions of men had said before consequences had taught them the contrary, and before the experience of what disunion would lead to had frightened them into full orthodoxy.

Meanwhile Stephen Gardiner, like Henry himself, was intensely Catholic in doctrine and practice, as opposed to the Lutheran and still more as opposed to the Calvinist. And this endeared him to Henry, though Henry dreaded the strength and activity of his character. Gardiner always stood for the defence of the old national traditions in religion, of the Mass of course, but also of the full doctrine of the Real Presence, and so down to the minor devotions of Catholic practice.

When the violent discussions broke out among Henry's Bishops, some of whom—led by Cranmer and under the protection of Cromwell—became more and more anti-Catholic in tone, Gardiner put all his weight into the scale to oppose the break-up. He was largely responsible for and, perhaps, in part framed the famous Six Articles which during all the last years of Henry's reign enforced Catholic doctrine and practice under heavy penalties.

On this account it was that when Henry died, in 1547, and that unscrupulous gang, first under Somerset and then under Northumberland, fell like harpies onto the remaining property of the Church and, to fill their pockets, thoroughly supported the religious revolutionaries, Gardiner was clearly a public danger to them; for he was the spokesman of what the mass of Englishmen felt.

They imprisoned him and they deprived him of his bishopric; and so he remained persecuted and a victim of the effort to impose a new religion by terror upon the English. He was naturally the hero of all that great bulk of the nation which detested the new revolutionary doctrines and which rose in armed rebellion throughout the land against the newfangled Protestant service. Gardiner's name became the symbol of the older and better state of things the return of which men so ardently desired.

We shall see how when the diseased little Edward was dead Mary took Gardiner out of the Tower and raised him to the highest political position in England, making him her Chancellor—that is, much more even than what we should call to-day Prime Minister. And Gardiner now, bore witness to the fullness of his faith. There was no process of recantation, still less any trace of political motive.

That which he had never thought possible, the presence of an anti-Catholic government in England—the destruction of the Mass—the unscrupulous despoiling of Guild property—the oversetting of all Shrines—the wanton destruction of Churches—had proved to him what the fruits of disunion might be. But for the schism, which he had approved, such things could not have come to pass; and now he was determined to undo the schism and worked with all his might for the restoration of England to the unity of Christendom, which he had the great privilege to see accomplished before he died. As he died he gave the famous cry, *Negavi cum Petro, exivi cum Petro, sed non flevi cum Petro*: "I denied as Peter did, I went out as Peter did, but I have not wept as Peter did."

He was fortunate indeed to live to such a moment; and fortunate, I think, also in dying before he could see all the good work swept away.

For he passed on the twelfth of November, 1555, overshadowed indeed by some dread of the future but not witnessing the breakdown which followed three years later on Mary's death. What overshadowed him was his fear of the results of the Spanish marriage. He had been again typically English in his stout resistance to that policy. It was he who had urged upon the Queen the advisability of marrying one of her own English nobles, and if Courteney had had a better character he would have carried his point.

This opposition to Mary's Spanish marriage put him in a minority in the Council and he had to give way. Indeed the marriage with Philip was solemnized in his own Cathedral and by Gardiner himself.

There is one last point to be made with regard to him, and that is his attitude towards the prosecutions of the revolutionaries for heresy rather than for treason. Because he was Chancellor, because he was Mary's right-hand man and the most prominent of the Catholic protagonists, the symbol of tradition in the national religion, he was until recently almost universally accused by our official historians of particular harshness and even cruelty in the treatment of the heretics after the new policy began.

Now what was his real attitude towards it? We have no need for reluctance in the matter. The government had a perfect right to treat a small rebel minority, which was working for the destruction of religion and of the Monarch as well, as public enemies; it was rather a matter of policy than of morals whether the rebels should be treated as heretics or as traitors. But was Gardiner as a fact prominent in the prosecutions? Was he a leading spirit in them? It may be doubted or even denied.

As Chancellor it was of course his business to preside over the affair; but it is to be remarked that he took pains to save men from the consequences of their error, that he personally helped some of those most in danger to escape from the country, and in his own great diocese there were no executions. That was due in part, of course, to the fact that the poison had not reached the western country parts over which that diocese extended; it was only virulent in London, one or two seaport towns and certain sections of East Anglia and the Home Counties.

But still, from all that we know of the nature of the man and of his policy in other things, we may fairly conclude that if he had had a free hand he would have been in favour of Philip of Spain's policy and not of that of the Council. He would, I think, had he had a free hand, have made a few examples by prosecuting for treason; but he would have prevented the wholesale prosecutions for heresy. For that was what Mary's Spanish husband had urged: to repress treason rather than heresy. But Paget and the council, to show their English independence, rejected the foreigner's counsel.

Such I say should be, I think, our general conclusion. But we must not run to the extreme of saying that he was an *overt* opponent to the policy of prosecuting and executing for heresy; he certainly was not that. When it was once undertaken he carried it out, and nothing by way of public pronouncement fell from him to show that he objected. He did not for instance openly oppose it as he had openly opposed the Spanish marriage.

Such was Stephen Gardiner; a character then most national, which more than any other helps us to grasp, when we are fully acquainted with it, the character of the time in which he lived, and especially the attitude of the normal Englishman in those difficult and confused days.

There was no one to succeed him; there was no other typical national figure to symbolize the reluctance and the distaste everywhere profoundly felt for the new and fanatical movement against the ancient national traditions of England. Had there been one such (one of similar authority and with as great a past), in the first years of Elizabeth's reign, Cecil would perhaps not have undertaken with the same success the evil work he did.

MARY TUDOR

MOST OF the leading characters of the English Reformation have been presented to modern readers in a distorted fashion. In the case of those who were the most important, such as Thomas Cromwell and William Cecil, this distortion results in a false impression of the whole movement. Mary Tudor, Henry VIII's eldest child and only legitimate daughter, was not one of those characters which mainly moulded the Reformation period one way or the other. She was more acted upon than acting; but as her character has been more distorted than that of any other it is both of interest and importance for our judgment of the time to get it right.

The reason that her character has been more distorted than any other is this: she was the most strongly orthodox Catholic of all the principal figures of the time. When she came to the throne she stood for the great mass of the nation in this respect, for the great mass of the nation was, of course, wholly Catholic in 1553 when she acceded, and could not imagine it could ever become anything else. It was under her government that the prosecution of the religious revolutionaries, who were also social and political revolutionaries, was carried out with the most activity. On these accounts the English writers, when England had become Protestant long after, tended to make Mary Tudor a more active figure than she was because they tended to make her villainess of the piece. A ridiculous picture was drawn of a vindictive fanatical woman, attempting to repress the universal dislike of Catholicism by a sort of reign of terror. Her short reign is still called, in the official English histories at Oxford and Cambridge, "the Marian Reaction," as though the English people were then progressing in a tide towards Protestantism and the short six years of Mary's reign were a mere abortive and cruel effort to check a great national movement.

All that, of course, is absurdly false: of all the falsehoods of our official history it is perhaps the one falsehood most widely divorced from reality.

There was no national movement towards Protestantism; the Queen was popular; the prosecution and execution of the religious revolutionaries excited no national protest.

But the curious thing is that those who should be the defenders of true, that is Catholic, history, have helped to perpetuate the legend by doing no more than answer individual points in it and not dealing with its falsity as a whole.

For instance, they point out that if Mary persecuted she was only acting according to the spirit of the time; that if she put to death a great number of Protestants, so under Elizabeth were put to death a great number of Catholics—and so on. They imply the whole time that the main thesis of their opponents is true, namely, that England was already Protestant or at least was divided into two halves—Protestant and Catholic; that the initiative in the executions proceeded from Mary herself, and that her government had no right to check rebellion.

When you meet the falsehood of an opponent by picking holes in the details of what he says, while still admitting his general thesis, you only confirm the error which he desires to propagate: the right way of meeting false propaganda is by the statement of the truth and the vigorous erection of a true picture which shall cancel the false one.

The true picture of Mary Tudor is that of a woman simple in character, like her mother, somewhat warped by isolation, devout, thoroughly virtuous, led of necessity by her all-powerful Council but in some points insisting upon her own will, and without too much judgment. She was also a woman suffering, like all Henry's children, from bad health and dying early; a woman who was thoroughly representative in her religion of the bulk of the nation, and yet who was somewhat out of touch with the spirit of the nation in important matters, such as that of her Spanish marriage. It is further true that had she lived a few years longer England would probably be Catholic to-day, and had she had a child England would certainly be Catholic to-day. For the English people had always loved her and always regarded her as their true Queen and would not have tolerated the rivalry of anyone against her descendants.

Mary Tudor was born in 1516, on February 18, when Henry and his wife Catherine of Aragon had been happily married for less than seven years, when the young King was still devoted to his wife and when everything was going well.

Queen Catherine had had great misfortunes in the matter of childbirth; children stillborn or dying immediately after birth, and one or two miscarriages. When therefore it was seen that the child would survive it was a matter of great rejoicing to the King and to the whole nation, of which she became a sort of idol. Henry hoped, of course, for a male heir, but as none came he and the nation took it for granted that the little Princess would ultimately become one of those great Queens who were so conspicuous a mark of the period, like her grandmother, Isabella of Castile.

Then came the tragedy of Henry's infatuation for Anne Boleyn. We shall never understand Mary's character unless we appreciate the fact that she grew up under the influence of that tragedy, just in those years when strong emotions are felt and the whole character is formed. She was a very intelligent, very well educated, sensitive child in her twelfth year, devoted to her mother and standing in affectionate awe of her father (who doted on her) when the first news of a sort which could be told to a child came to her of Anne's disgraceful power over the King.

She was in her fourteenth year when the great trial was held under Wolsey and Campeggio in London by which Henry hoped to obtain his divorce from her mother, Queen Catherine. She was already quite able to understand everything that was happening and to burn with indignation against the abominable way in which her mother was being treated. She was a woman grown, in her eighteenth year, when Anne Boleyn was crowned Queen and was therefore in a position to heap indignity and insult not only on the legitimate Queen (who was now exiled from Court) but on the legitimate heiress to the English throne, Mary herself.

It was at such an age—eighteen—that Mary saw the illegitimate child of her mother's rival—the baby Elizabeth—proclaimed heiress to England and herself legally bastardized. Finally, when she lost her chief support by her mother's death, she was within six weeks of her twentieth birthday.

All that youth of hers had been passed in the one preoccupation of the shameful affair which was bitterly disastrous and humiliating to her. Her father would have renewed his relations of affection with her if he could, but he was too weak, and Anne Boleyn always interfered. Henceforth she was utterly lonely and could depend for counsel and advice upon no one in the kingdom, only upon her cousin the great Emperor Charles V, sixteen years older than herself and the head of her mother's family.

She stood out as best she could against the schism, but in her bewilderment and under the strain of perpetual pressure, gave way, and in a tragic moment admitted Henry's supremacy, though in her heart of course she never accepted it.

So long as Henry lived, that is, till the year 1547, by which time Mary

Tudor was a woman of nearly thirty-one and already marked by permanent grief, she remained in this anomalous position; and further troubles began with the accession to power of the gang of harpies who looted the Royal domain and the Church under her little half-brother, Edward VI. They tried to interfere with her practise of her religion and indeed she was only maintained in that by the active intervention of her cousin the Emperor.

When the diseased little lad died, an effort was made by Cranmer, Cecil, Dudley and the rest to substitute Lady Jane Grey for Mary's legitimate claim to the throne. They tried to trap Mary into coming to London, where they would certainly have imprisoned her and probably put her to death. She showed the greatest courage. Her cousin the Emperor advised her to take refuge on the Continent. She refused to do so. She made a prodigious ride of two days away from London eastward and there was an enthusiastic popular rising in her favour which destroyed the plans of the conspirators.

But here came the crisis. She could not reign without the great nobles, the very same people who had conspired against her. They were too powerful for her to do without them. She did, indeed, release from prison and take for her principal adviser the great Bishop Gardiner, but she had to admit to the Council much the same sort of men as those who had been guilty of the orgy of loot of Church property under her little brother's nominal reign. She had to accept as an accomplished fact the millions they enjoyed out of the robbery of the Church, and she could not but feel all the time that her position was one of compromise.

Popular though she was with the mass of the English people and highly accomplished, she was handicapped in person and with no experience of the world, and had had little training in the judgment of character. She was, as I have said, of bad health, she was short, prematurely aged (in her thirty-eighth year but looking fifteen years older), she had a rough deep voice almost like a man's, a head too big for her body, and altogether an unimpressive presence; and in her relations with the men and women about her she was much too ready to believe in the good and to doubt the evil.

This was especially the case in her relations with her younger illegitimate sister Elizabeth. That young woman, only twenty when Mary came to the throne, was the figurehead at once of the small revolutionary party in religion and of all those thousands of newly enriched men among whom were now divided the spoils of the Church. They accepted in Parliament (which was entirely composed of their class) the reconciliation with Rome, but only on condition that they could keep the monastic lands; and each of them would certainly have felt more secure in his ill-gotten gains with Elizabeth instead of Mary on the throne.

At the very beginning of her reign the matter of her marriage went wrong. It was imperative that she should be married soon, that there should be an heir to the throne. Gardiner, her Chancellor and chief minister, advised a marriage with a semi-royal cousin, Courteney, the only suitable native candidate. But he was quite a young man, dissolute and therefore repulsive to her; she decided against Gardiner's advice, and after much hesitation and repeated prayer she determined to marry her cousin Philip, the Emperor's son, to whom had been given the Kingdom of Spain and the Netherlands: a man fifteen years younger than herself.

This marriage was somewhat unpopular throughout England but was especially so in London and the Home Counties. It was most unpopular with the rich, because throughout Europe the quarrel of the Reformation was now long established and Philip, standing as he did as the head of the Catholic cause, seemed to endanger the continued possession by the new millionaires of the Church lands which they had stolen in England. The discontent was fanned by the French King and his Ambassador in London, because the marriage would increase the power of Spain, France's rival at the time. There was an insurrection which very nearly succeeded, backed with French money and French guns. It was launched under the promise that there should be a French invasion in aid of it.

This insurrection, called Wyatt's Rebellion, was put down; but Mary was far too merciful on this occasion. She spared her young half-sister Elizabeth who was undoubtedly mixed up in the affair, and she believed Elizabeth when that Princess declared herself whole-heartedly Catholic and disavowed the religious revolutionaries. But those revolutionaries were now not only religious, they were also political revolutionaries and many of them social revolutionaries as well. During the six years of Edward VI's nominal reign they had had their way, they had tasted power and it gave them courage. Moreover the sincerely religious enthusiasts among them had an intensity of feeling which made them exceedingly dangerous.

Philip, now King of England side by side with the Queen, was—on the advice of his father the Emperor—strongly in favour of dealing with the danger as a purely civil and political one; his Chaplain was ordered to preach a sermon advising toleration, his idea and that of the Emperor being that the revolutionaries should be dealt with as traitors rather than as heretics.

But the Council, which in those days was the real governing power, was exasperated by seeing a foreign Prince acting as their rival and, *largely out of opposition to him*, they determined upon the opposite policy—to which Mary herself was quite willing to accede. They would try to put down the revolutionaries as heretics, rather than as traitors.

When, therefore, a sermon was preached by one of the fanatics praying for the Queen's death, instead of getting the culprit hanged for treason, which would probably have been the wiser course, they proceeded to inaugurate a policy of prosecutions for heresy. For one man who would have risked death under the infamous charge of treason there were ten who were ready to offer themselves as martyrs for various forms of intense anti-Catholicism, principally Calvinist.

Therefore the Council's original hope that a few executions would be sufficient to suppress the revolutionary movement failed; and though the executions were restricted to a comparatively small part of England they were numerous and continuous. They were especially numerous in London, which was the one great town of the kingdom, the one place where opinion could be easily inflamed and where also was the chief strength of this small religious minority. The north and west were almost untouched and the Midlands were not seriously disaffected.

In this way the last half of Mary's reign was filled with the perpetual attempt to suppress the revolutionary movement as a religious rather than as a political thing. A few more years of persecution would almost certainly have been successful, but it was cut off short by Mary's death at the end of 1558, when she had reigned only five and a half years.

It is significant that the chief promoter of these burnings was Paget, a man personally indifferent in religion but himself one of the new millionaires, filled with Church loot. It is significant also that the Council was so determined in its policy, in order to show its power against Philip, that its members even took advantage of Mary's illness to try to put to death one of her own favourites, whom she with difficulty saved. But all the while it must be remembered that Mary herself remained personally popular, especially with the poorer people, with whom she mixed humbly and charitably, while her undoubted position as legitimate in birth and true Queen was enthusiastically acclaimed to the end.

Philip soon after the marriage had left for the Continent, where his presence was necessary in the war against France. The Queen was supposed to be with child. Everything was made ready for the birth, but it was a false alarm; she was not pregnant but suffering from the dropsy from which she died. Her death was very holy and beautiful. She died as her mother had died, hearing the Mass which was being said in her death-chamber in the early hours of a dark winter's morning; and it is pathetic but pleasant to remember that as she died she said that angel children were about her bed.

With her death the whole gang immediately seized power, using Elizabeth whom she had spared and whom she had regarded as her successor, because she had been deceived by the violent protestations of Catholic loyalty on the part of that Princess.

With the death of Mary and the advent of Elizabeth began that slow and ultimately successful effort to drive the Mass out of England and destroy Catholicism in the people. But Mary died under the impression that the situation had been met, and that the national religion, to which the great majority of Englishmen still adhered, was no longer in grave or imminent peril.

QUEEN ELIZABETH

THE INTEREST of Queen Elizabeth to the historian is mainly biographical; but it has also the interest of a myth.

The interest is mainly biographical because she was of very little effect upon the history of her time. We do not find any great political events produced by her will or her intelligence and there is nothing important in the Europe of her time or the England of her time of which we can say, "This was done by Elizabeth."

But the woman herself is so interesting, not only as a pathological case but as an example of suffering and intelligence combined, of a warped temperament and all that goes with it, that, biographically, she is a first-rate subject and one which, it may be added, has never been properly dealt with. There is no one well-known book which gives an even approximately true picture of Elizabeth; at least, none in the English language.

The reason of this is due to the presence of that other interest in her character, the myth. What may be called "The Elizabethan Myth" is only now beginning to break down, and it was during the nineteenth century an article of faith in England (and, through England, elsewhere). It is one of the most perfect modern examples of its kind in all the range of history. It is a sort of creative and vital falsehood, radiating its effects upon all the details of the time, and putting in the wrong light pretty well everything that happened.

The Elizabethan myth may be stated thus:

"In the second half of the sixteenth century England had the good fortune to be governed by a woman of strong will, powerful intelligence and excellent judgment, whose power was supreme. Her people adored her, and produced in her time and largely under her influence the greatest figures in every sphere: Literature, Architecture, Foreign Politics and the rest. She chose her ministers with admirable skill and they served her with corresponding faithfulness. In consequence of all this the Great Queen led the nation through paths of increasing prosperity; it grew wealthier and wealthier as her reign proceeded, more and more powerful abroad, founding colonies and establishing that command of the sea which England has never since lost. In religion she wisely represented the strong Protestantism of her people in hatred of which a few venomous rebels—shamefully allied with foreigners—attacked her reign and even her life. However, she easily triumphed over them all and died full of glory, leaving her name as that of the greatest of the English sovereigns."

There in brief is the "Elizabethan Myth," and a more monstrous scaffolding of poisonous nonsense has never been foisted on posterity. I use the word "poisonous" not at random, not as a mere epithet of abuse, but with a full sense of its accuracy; for this huge falsehood which might be merely absurd in another connection has had, applied to English history, all the effect that a poison has upon a living body. It has interfered with the proper scale of history, it has twisted, altered and denied the most obvious historical truths and has given Englishmen and even the world at large a false view of our past.

The myth is now beginning to break down. It could not survive detailed and critical work. Moreover, I perceive a danger that in its breakdown there will be too strong a reaction the other way and that men when they find out how they have been duped will run to the opposite extreme, and perhaps come to believe that Elizabeth was insignificant.

Whatever she was she was not that. Her position was weak, but she herself was not weak.

The truth about Elizabeth is this. She was the puppet or figurehead of the group of new millionaires established upon the loot of religion begun in her father's time. They had at their head the unique genius of William Cecil, who, in spite of dangerous opposition, accomplished what might have seemed the impossible task of digging up the Catholic Faith by the roots from English soil, stamping out the Mass, and shepherding the younger generation of a reluctant people into a new religious mood.

Throughout her life Elizabeth was thwarted in each political effort she made; she felt the check of her masters and especially Cecil as a horse feels the bridle. She never had her will in matters of State.

In personal history the truth about Elizabeth is that she was a woman of strong will and warped by desperately bad bodily health, almost certainly by a secret abnormality which forbade her to bear children. This wretched health, to which half a dozen times in her life she nearly succumbed, partly accounted for a mind also diseased on the erotic side. It is not a pleasant subject, and not one on which I can dwell at length in these pages, but it must be very strongly emphasized for it accounts for all her intimate life and all that was most characteristic of her from her fifteenth year.

Her relations with men were continual, but they were not normal and they were the more scandalous for that. Like others who have suffered the same tragic disease of perversion in mind and body it seemed to increase upon her with age. Already within sight of the grave and approaching her seventieth year she was shamefully associated with one whom she had taken up as a lad, a young fellow nearly thirty-three years her junior. Her intellect was high and piercing, she had real wit, very full instruction in many languages, and her will, in spite of perpetual rebuffs, remained strong to the end, though woefully impotent to carry into effect.

No one chafed more or suffered more under the domination of others than Elizabeth, and no one has had to accept it more thoroughly. She had, on this side of the intelligence and of the will, only one weakness, but that so exaggerated that it was hardly sane. She insisted upon flattery, and particularly upon flattery which was so exaggerated as to be absurd. She certainly was not taken in by it, but she seems to have had a maniac appetite for it, liking it the more the more she knew it to be absurd. When she had long been dried up and wizened, with a skin like parchment, already old but looking a far older ruin than she was, she insisted upon her flatterers addressing her as though she were a woman of great beauty in the bloom of youth.

Elizabeth was never beautiful, and after the age of thirty she became repulsive. In that year she lost all her reddish hair through an illness and had to supply the loss by a reddish wig. Her complexion had never been good since the first years of her youth; but she carried herself with dignity and in spite of her physical disabilities her energy and vivacity of mind certainly made her a good companion. So far from her reign being the foundation of England's modern power or anything of that sort it was a period during which, as Thorold Rogers has proved, wealth was continually declining, towns shrinking in population and land going out of cultivation. It is true that a race of bold seamen arose contemporaneously with that reign, but they were no more remarkable than the captains of other nations in Europe at the same time and they nearly all bore the taint of theft and murder. They were slave-dealers and pirates, secretly supported by the powerful men of the State; Elizabeth could not but feel the shame which their piracies brought upon her in the eyes of her fellow sovereigns, and yet could not avoid taking part in the proceeds of the disgraceful business. For Cecil's principle was to let such men as Hawkins, Drake and the rest rob indiscriminately, to disavow them in public, to apologize for their acts, sometimes even to compensate the victims in part, but to keep the gains of their misdeeds—much the greater part of which went into the pockets of the men who held political power, while the criminal agents themselves were left with no more than a small commission. The only military effort of the reign, that in Holland, was a ridiculous failure; the only effort at colonization was the equally ridiculous failure of Virginia.

In religion Elizabeth inclined at first to that witty, cynical scepticism of the Renaissance, the spirit of many intellectuals of the time in which she was steeped. She was ready in youth to adopt any outward conformity required of her. Calvinist as a girl, under the rule of those who were despoiling the State after her father's death, she was quite ready to profess enthusiasm for the Catholic Church, as we have seen, when her sister Mary was on the throne; but secretly enjoying the influence given her by the fact that the religious revolutionaries looked to her as a counterweight against her sister and as one who, when they could put her upon the throne, would make certain of their ill-gotten gains at the expense of the Catholic Church.

As she grew older she developed a certain measure of carefully concealed piety—her private prayers prove that. It is a feature not uncommon in people who are tortured by some abnormality in their intimate life. It is a sort of refuge for them.

Her mature sympathies were, of course, however vaguely, with the Catholic Church. All the great monarchs among whom she wished to be counted as an equal were struggling to maintain the old civilization of Europe, of which the Catholic Faith was the creator and the supreme expression. Philip of Spain, the head of the Catholic movement, had saved her life; she had long respected and depended upon him until, in spite of her and in spite of himself Cecil had turned him into an enemy. She tried hard for an understanding with the Papacy; she detested the new Anglican Establishment which Cecil had put up and of which she was, in spite of herself, the political head.

It was one of those very few minor points on which she was allowed to have her own way that she refused to call herself as her father had called himself, "Vicar of Christ and Supreme Head of the Church on Earth." She detested the idea of a married clergy and always refused to receive the wives of the new Establishment. She would, had she been allowed, have sent emissaries to the Council of Trent; and though, of course, the thing cannot be proved and is pure conjecture, I have thought it certain enough that she would, in the case of a successful Catholic rising, had the Catholic emigrants and their supporters been able to bring a sufficient force into England, have joined what was still the religion of the majority of her subjects though cowed and terrorized by the reign of Cecil's government. The fall of that government would have been indeed a release for her.

As examples of the way in which she was "run" by those who were her masters, I will take four leading cases out of a very great number which might be quoted:

1. She had personally given her Royal assurance to the Spanish Minister that the Spanish treasure ships bearing the pay for Alva's soldiers in the Netherlands, the ships which had taken refuge from pirates in English harbours, should be released and the money taken under safeguards to its proper destination. Cecil simply over-ruled her. He ordered the money to be kept and confiscated in spite of her, and *his* orders, not *hers*, were obeyed.

2. Again, she desired to save Norfolk. Three separate times she interfered to prevent the execution. She was overruled. That unfortunate cousin of hers was put to death, but his blood is not upon her head; it is upon Cecil's.

3. She tried to recall Drake just before the open declaration of war with Spain; no one thought of obeying her orders in the matter.

4. The supreme example is the case of Mary, Queen of Scots. The murder—for it was a murder—was accomplished against her will. Our official historians have perpetually repeated that her agony at hearing of Mary's death was feigned: that is, false. It was genuine. The signing of the warrant had indeed been wrung out of her, but that did not mean that the warrant would be put into execution. It was put into execution in spite of her, in order that she should be made responsible, willing or unwilling.

One might add to the list at any length. Her paramour, Leicester, did what he willed in Holland without consulting her, keeping a Royal State which she flamed against impotently. Her later paramour, Essex, kept the loot of Cadiz and defied, without fear of consequences, her bitter anger at finding herself deprived of her Royal right to the proceeds of an act of war undertaken in her name. She never desired the death of Essex; it was Robert Cecil, the second Cecil, who was responsible for Essex's death. Not only would she have prevented it if she could, but one may fairly say that she died of it.

And to what a death did the unhappy woman come! A death of madness and despair. The late Hugh Benson wrote a most powerful pamphlet contrasting that death with the holy, happy, and pious death of Mary.

She crouched on the ground for hours, one may say for days, refusing to speak, with her finger in her mouth, after having suffered horrible illusions—thinking that she had an iron band pressing round her head and on one occasion seeing herself in a sort of vision as a little figure surrounded with flames. She passed unannealed, unabsolved, and it is one of the most horrible stories in history.

Nevertheless we must admit her greatness. A warped, distorted, diseased greatness, but greatness none the less.

And there is another note on which I would conclude, a note of warning which is always necessary when one is correcting a false impression in history. The issue was not clear-cut. It must ever be so when the real power is in one hand, the nominal power in another. It is the nominal power which impresses men and even those who exercise the real power half believe in it, and those who exercise the nominal power also more than half believe in it. Cecil would never have told you that he was the real master of England, and, even though upon a strict examination of conscience he would have had to admit it, he still regarded himself a minister and servant. And she herself, Elizabeth, was of course filled with the idea of her office to the end, that ideal of monarchy which men still held. Yet it was under her that the monarchy of England began to fall to pieces so rapidly that within half a lifetime after her death the rich taxpayers not only rose in rebellion successfully against the Crown, but put their Monarch, her second successor, to death.

With that event, the beheading of Charles I, the old English monarchy came to an end, and it remained nothing but a simulacrum of itself. Government had passed to the gentry and to their two great committees, the House of Lords and the House of Commons.

Some day I suppose a true life of Elizabeth will be written in the English language, but, as I have said, we have not had it yet. There is here a great opportunity for the younger historians, and one of them I think will take it.

MARY STUART

THE FIRST thing to appreciate about Mary Stuart is that she was the legitimate Queen of England after the death of Mary Tudor.

Each of the other very important points in connection with her—her fascination, her individual character, her follies, her courage, her later heroism and what may almost be called her martyrdom—all the particular historical problems connected with her career—such as the authenticity of the Casket Letters, or her real attitude towards the so-called Babington Plot—have their rightful place; but we must beware of putting them in the wrong order.

Protestant history and, therefore, our official history, such as it is taught in the English Universities and has spread throughout English Literature in textbooks and fiction, gave a thoroughly wrong perspective of this as of every other essential matter in the English Reformation.

One would gather from this official version and its effects in general literature that Mary was a sort of untoward accident, interfering with the normal process of English political life in the later sixteenth century. Her presence and her claims are represented as being dreaded by the England of her day as might be dreaded the presence of an alien body in an organism, which alien body that organism must get rid of if it is to survive.

The truth is just the other way. Mary was regarded by the general opinion of the time as the woman who ought by right to be Queen of England. She was certainly legitimate, while Elizabeth, her rival, was as certainly illegitimate by all the moral canons of the day. She stood in her later years not only for the Catholic religion, to which the mass of Englishmen still adhered in general sympathy at least, but also for the principle then held as something of awful sanctity—the principle of the Blood Royal: the right of men and women to rule by descent and primogeniture.

It is essential in history to read every period according to the spirit of that period, even when that spirit has disappeared or has been so modified that we moderns have difficulty in understanding its strength. In most discussions of Queen Elizabeth's reign, which was really the reign of the Cecils, that essential point is overlooked. But, indeed, the fault is the commonest one in all dealings with the past. It is the same fault which makes people ridicule, instead of trying to understand, the violence of theological controversy in the Eastern Empire, or the sentiment of loyalty in service which was the cement of the feudal system. In the same way some historian of the future might misunderstand the whole of the nineteenth century by ridiculing as absurd and incomprehensible the sentiment of nationalism or the ideals of democracy.

Mary Stuart was, in the eyes of her contemporaries, the legitimate Queen of England, for the following reason: she was the senior legitimate descendant of an English King, to wit Henry VII, the father of Henry VIII.

Henry VII had three children who survived to have children themselves. These three children of Henry VII were Henry, who became Henry VIII; Margaret, who became Queen of Scotland; and Mary, who became Queen of France and afterwards Duchess of Suffolk. Henry VIII had two legitimate children who survived him: Mary Tudor and little Edward. Edward came first because he was a male; Mary Tudor was the next in succession according to all the ideas and morals of the time.

Henry VIII also had two illegitimate children; one, the Duke of Richmond, died young; the other, Elizabeth, survived. She was illegitimate in the eyes of Christendom generally according to all the ideas of the time because she was born while the legitimate wife of Henry was still alive, the marriage not having been declared null by competent authority but only at the orders of Henry himself.

Therefore, when Mary Tudor was dead one had to look to the descendants of Henry VII's two daughters to find the senior representative of the Blood Royal. It is true that Henry VIII had made a Will in which he named his successors, after his own children (wherein he included Elizabeth). These successors whom he named were the descendants of Mary, Duchess of Suffolk, his younger sister, and he said nothing about the descendants of Margaret, his elder one. It is also true that this Will was given the force of a Statute by the King in Parliament. But it is false to regard the Crown of England as dependent upon a Parliamentary title. That theory was invented long after; nor could a King legally name his successor at his own caprice though it is true that the desires of a monarch in this matter did weigh heavily at the time.

What counted most with all men was the sanctity of the Blood Royal and the rights of seniority. Since Margaret, Queen of Scotland, was the elder daughter of Henry VII, her descendants had the prior claim. The descendants of Mary, Duchess of Suffolk, were the Ladies Grey and it will be remembered that the elder of them, Lady Jane Grey, was made a claimant for the throne on that account, because, although she was of the junior branch, she was Protestant. Of the elder sister Margaret, the first descendant was her son, the King of Scotland. But he was dead, and the second was that son's only child, Mary Stuart. Mary Stuart was therefore by all the ideas of the time the person who had a right to be Queen of England when Mary Tudor died. On that the whole of her story turns.

People felt about it just as to-day they feel about an election. A man who has received a majority of votes in the electoral college to be President of the United States or to be a member of Parliament for an English constituency we regard as the legitimate holder of that office, and anyone who should try to hold it in opposition to him with a minority of votes we should regard as having no legitimate right, however much we might approve of him in other ways. In the sixteenth century all the morals of the time took it for granted that the ruler of a monarchic country should be the senior representative of the Blood Royal.

Now as against this indefeasible claim of Mary Stuart's there went the following points in practice:

First, she was not English. She was born to the throne of Scotland, she had been brought up in France, she was an alien; for Scotland in those days was regarded as alien to England and even as one of the chief enemies of England.

Again, because Scotland always allied herself with France in order to preserve her independence against her neighbour England, Mary Stuart had been married to the heir of the French king, and during the brief reign of that heir (who died a few months after his succession) she was actually Queen of France. At the moment when Mary Tudor died she was living in France as the wife of this young heir. To have made her Queen of England then would have meant the probable amalgamation, in the near future, of Scotland, England and France under one crown. That would have been a loss of national independence for England.

Also there could have been no question of the French court releasing her and bringing her over to England, though she was made, of course, to affirm her rightful claim at once.

Further, it was all important to Philip, the King of Spain, of whom the

French were the dangerous rivals and enemies, to prevent French influence from growing in England. Therefore, he strongly supported Elizabeth who was on the spot, and whom Cecil, with Philip behind him, put upon the throne.

When Mary Stuart's young husband the King of France died she was only in her eighteenth year. She was only henceforward Queen Dowager of France, and there could be no question of an amalgamation of the two thrones. Still, she was French bred and represented French influence, and her mother of the great French house of Guise had been the Regent in Scotland, so she was still a thoroughly foreign claimant in English eyes, though the legitimate claimant. And that feeling was emphasized when she went back to Scotland as Queen the next year, landing some months before her nineteenth birthday.

So strong was the feeling that her claim might succeed that Cecil was all for getting hold of her and keeping her prisoner; and an attempt was made to seize her as she sailed past the eastern coasts of England on her way north. The attempt failed through a fog, but luck would have it that Cecil had his way in the long run after all and Mary became his captive. The way this happened was as follows:

When Mary landed in Scotland the religious revolution which, as we have seen, had made some little progress in England, though not much, which in Germany had swept everything into violent turmoil, and which in France was soon to bring about prolonged civil war, had in Scotland achieved a very great measure of success. Calvinism had become the enthusiastic creed of a minority, burning with zeal and determined to succeed. The majority were not similarly zealous for the defence of the Church, which in Scotland had become thoroughly corrupt; and the great Scottish nobles who had everything in their hands supported the religious revolution because it gave them the power to loot the Church and the monarchy wholesale.

Into this anarchy Mary was plunged. For seven years her invincible courage still maintained her as Queen; but her temperament ruined what small chances she had of maintaining her position. We must remember in her favour that she was a woman of especial fascination which in a sense she exercises to this day; and that yet it was her misfortune to be married first to a sickly boy even younger than herself who died before she was eighteen and next by her own judgment and error to her cousin Darnley, a debauched and worthless character. She was accused, falsely, of having taken part in the murder of Darnley. The act was really that of the rebel

Scotch nobles, but it was widely believed that she was guilty of it and still more widely believed (it is still a problem) that she was at any rate cognizant of what was in the wind.

It was her temperament again that made her fall a victim to Bothwell, one of her own great nobles in Scotland, a masterly man to whom she succumbed. Though she was the representative of Catholicism she married him with Calvinistic rites, and as he was universally regarded as at least one of the murderers of her first husband the scandal was enormous. She was imprisoned, she escaped, she was defeated; and in 1568, her twenty-sixth year, she escaped, unarmed and without resources, over the border into England—trusting to the promised protection of Elizabeth. From that moment of course she was in Cecil's power.

She was held first virtually, then actually, as a prisoner, and so remained for nearly twenty years.

Now during all those twenty years Mary Stuart's position in the eyes of Europe and in the eyes of many Englishmen was that of the legitimate Queen of England, imprisoned by the government of a usurper. With that attitude the bulk of Englishmen did not agree. They were used to the Tudor dynasty; they had been familiar throughout her life with Elizabeth who was now upon the throne and had been for now ten years the figure-head, at least, of government, and a vigorous figure-head, though really ruled by Cecil.

Yet there was a large minority of Englishmen who felt so strongly in the matter that they would have put Mary Stuart upon the throne or, at any rate, have insisted upon her succeeding Elizabeth; for it was getting more and more certain that Elizabeth was incapable of having an heir.

There was a rebellion in Mary's favour which was crushed by Cecil's government with the utmost barbarity; and thenceforward her immediate cause was lost. An effort to marry her to the young Duke of Norfolk, who, though a strong Protestant, represented the older nobility, was discovered by Cecil and was used by him as a pretext for putting Norfolk to death and for affirming his triumph over his rivals; and thenceforward Mary remained not only a closer prisoner than ever but one whom Cecil also planned to put to death in her turn.

Cecil's main reason for getting Mary out of the way was the fact that he was the head of the clique of new millionaires who could not be certain of their continued power unless Catholicism were crushed; and a second reason was that, through the growing Protestantism of Scotland, Cecil and the English government could become the protectors of Scotland, which kingdom this policy in the long run wholly subjected to English influence, until at last, long after Cecil's death, the two countries were merged into one, and Scotland—though Scotsmen to this day will never admit it—became but a province of English rule. For a long time past, as everybody knows, Scotland and England, united by their common Protestantism and by a thousand consequent ties, have become one nation.

Now to put Mary Stuart to death was an enormity. Yet the demand for it was present and open and Cecil worked for it with all his might against every moral obstacle, and finally succeeded. A pretext had to be found, and was found in the following manner:

Cecil's man Walsingham, his head spy and extremely efficient at his trade, sent an *agent provocateur* (what is called in modern English slang a "nark") to stir up one more of the innumerable plots against Elizabeth abroad. This agent, a renegade Catholic of the name of Giffard, egged on a group of hot-headed people, refugee Catholics in France with a rich and romantic young man called Babington as their nominal head, to plot the release of Mary Stuart from captivity, to put her on the throne of England and, at least, to constrain and, if necessary, to kill Elizabeth.

To devise rebellion against the reigning sovereign, and especially to envisage her death, was high treason; and the essential of Walsingham's action was to make out a case that Mary Stuart was party to the plot, and, particularly, to the death of Elizabeth. In order to make out this case a system was devised whereby letters passing from the conspirators to Mary Stuart and from her to all in the outside world could be read without her knowledge.

A go-between was suborned who was supposed to be a faithful adherent of Mary's but was really a traitor in the pay of Walsingham and his officials. In one of these letters, sent by Babington, allusion was made to the killing of Elizabeth. Mary replied to it. Did she in that reply take part in the project for the killing of the reigning English Queen?

Walsingham said she did. But the draft of her letter, which remained in Walsingham's possession, he never dared produce. It came out that, at least, one very important sentence in this letter had been deliberately forged by Philips, one of Walsingham's officials, with Walsingham's knowledge and was not written by Mary at all; it is the sentence in which she was made to ask for a list of the names of the men who were to do the deed. It is therefore presumable that Walsingham's accusation was false and that Mary never consented to the death of her cousin. She herself always vehemently denied it; she repeatedly challenged her prosecutors to produce the original drafts of the letters, which they refused to do. On their unsupported word she was condemned to death.

But Elizabeth appreciated what her responsibility would be in the eyes of all Europe, and what an abominable thing it was to bring an anointed sovereign and her own cousin and legitimate heir—for that matter the true Queen of England—to the scaffold. But Cecil was too powerful for Elizabeth; he was her master. The warrant had been signed, but Elizabeth had not given her assent to its being acted upon. Cecil took that responsibility upon himself, and, without Elizabeth's permission, had Mary Stuart beheaded on February 8, 1587.

The outrage raised a prodigious storm throughout Christendom. Philip of Spain launched the Armada against England to avenge it, and the Armada failed. All this group of events, ending in this failure of the Armada, made up the decisive and final crisis and success of the English Reformation. Thenceforward Cecil's increasingly successful plan was secure, and there could be no going back.

Very much more follows upon the tremendous business of Mary's violent death at the hands of the English government, the most important of which was perhaps the precedent which it gave against all the morals and ideas of the time, for the trial of a sovereign by subjects—a precedent with a tragic result for her grandson Charles I.

There runs then through the whole of Mary Stuart's story a group of intertwining threads which we may tabulate as follows. First, she was the representative of legitimacy and her tragedy put an end to the hitherto unchallenged claim in morals of the Blood Royal to rule. Next, she was the symbol of Catholicism in Great Britain, and her tragedy marked the defeat of Catholicism. Third, that tragedy meant the gradual absorption of Scotland as a nation under the influence of England.

Mary Stuart's son, James, whom she had not seen since he was a baby, was brought up a Calvinist through Cecil's influence and kept in the pay of Cecil's government. He shamefully acquiesced in his mother's death, and had his reward by being introduced to the English throne on the death of Elizabeth by Cecil's son Robert. He reigned as James I of England and James VI of Scotland, uniting the two nations under one head.

The whole story of this unfortunate woman remains and will remain full of unsolved problems. Mary Stuart will always be for some a martyr, for others a criminal, so long as the religious passions which centre round her name survive. The authenticity of the Casket Letters, to which I have alluded and which were supposed to prove her complicity with Bothwell, in the murder of Darnley, are still debated and perhaps will always be debated; and it is not the least tragic element in this tragedy that a complete and certain historical account of it still remains impossible.

WILLIAM CECIL

WILLIAM CECIL, who is better known as Lord Burghley, the title he took after clinching his great success in the middle of his career, was the author of Protestant England. One might almost call him the creator of modern England as a whole, for he stands at the root of the Church of England— the typical central religious institution following on the English Reformation; and it was under his rule that the seeds were sown of all that later developed into what is now the English political and social system.

It has often been remarked that England, more than any other European country, is cut off from her past. When England became Protestant she became a new thing and the old Catholic England of the thousand years before the Reformation is, to the Englishman after the Reformation, a foreign country. Now, the true artisan of that prodigious change was William Cecil, Lord Burghley.

Thomas Cromwell was the man who achieved the breach with Rome and who launched England out onto the beginning of the adventure, but William Cecil was the man who by his own genius and that of his son Robert—did the essential work of changing England from a Catholic to a Protestant country. It was he who eradicated the Faith from the English mind, it was he who prevented the succour of Catholic England by the power of Catholic Europe outside; it was he who instituted and maintained a reign of terror, the long endurance of which at last crushed out the Mass from English soil.

The false official history which has been taught so long ascribes what was really the action of Burghley to Queen Elizabeth. A false legend has been created with the object of exalting the character of that unhappy and distorted woman, but in truth she was but a figurehead, and it was William Cecil who during her reign moulded events to his will.

His was a very great political genius. The genius was set in a despicable character—mean, sly, avaricious and thoroughly false; morally he was a shrivelled soul corresponding to his little wizened body and face, but intellectually he was of the highest stature. To that unique intelligence of his was added an untiring industry and prodigious memory which between them left him in the period of his rise and power without a rival.

For he was in the midst of men bent upon the loot of the Church, upon pleasure, upon intriguing for places at Court, for salaries, and for fragment after fragment of the Royal fortune which they were dilapidating. None of them did any work unless it can be called work to pursue such ends. William Cecil worked all his life, with an iron will and a grasp of detail unparalleled in his time and hardly equalled before or since.

He had also an invincible tenacity, pursuing an original plan unswervingly and moulding to it any passing event. He had a profound knowledge of men, choosing his servants with skill and playing upon the weaknesses of all around him. He acted admirably; he could nearly always take a victim in, and the "old fox," as they nick-named him towards the end of his career, won nearly every conflict in which he was engaged.

He was without joy, and one may fairly say without religion. His motive was not hatred of the Catholic Church such as we find in Cranmer or in his own servant and head spy, Walsingham, the chief of his intelligence department. He destroyed the Church in England because he desired to confirm his own wealth and that of the clique of which he was the head, the new millionaires who had risen upon the booty of the monasteries, the bishoprics and all the rest.

He himself was not, oddly enough, a direct thief of Church land; the huge fortune of the Cecils which has kept them an important family even to this day came from the betrayal of colleagues, the enjoyment of lucrative posts, and all that can be done by unscrupulous men in power to their own enrichment. The lands they held were largely Church lands, but at second hand. The Cecils had no considerable grant that I can remember out of the original loot. Yet were they, and William Cecil their founder, the typical and representative heads of all that new wealth which arose on the ruins of religion in England.

William Cecil was, like Gardiner, of middle-class rank by birth. His father was what we should call to-day a permanent official in the government service—that is, he held a post in the establishment of Henry VIII. William's grandfather, the father of the official, had kept a hotel in Stamford, which is a town standing on the great Roman road running north from London; it is about ninety miles from the capital. Close to Stamford town, on the hill to the south of it, was the convent of Burghley, out of the ruins of which was later erected the magnificent palace which the family still holds and from which William Cecil took his title.

Henry VIII's official put the lad to Cambridge when he was fifteen years of age, just after Thomas Cromwell had broken with the Papacy. He did not rise very rapidly; he was nearly thirty before the father of his second wife introduced him to the Protector Somerset, the uncle of Edward VI and the man who attempted to impose Calvinism upon England during that little Prince's brief reign. He became Somerset's secretary, knowing all his secrets and keeping all his papers.

Then came his chance. After he had been secretary to Somerset for rather less than two years another member of the gang who were running the unfortunate little child-King, to wit Dudley, plotted to make himself supreme and to oust Somerset. Somerset in his peril turned to his secretary, and was aghast to find that he had been betrayed. The details of the betrayal we do not know, but we do know that William Cecil suddenly jumped from a good moderate position of what we should call to-day, perhaps £800 a year, to very great wealth. And, what is more, his patron, to whom he had betrayed his old master, made him secretary to the Council, that is, made him the man who kept all the State papers and knew all the State secrets. In that position, his wealth, of course, continued to increase.

Although he had conspired against Mary with the rest of the Council he managed to save himself. He outwardly conformed to the national religion during the Catholic Queen's reign, and he used to make a parade of carrying an enormous pair of rosary beads to emphasize his zeal. Then, when Mary died in 1558, it was he who got Elizabeth on to the throne, and she remained for the next twenty years wholly dependent upon his vast political capacity. It was he who suggested the gradual plan for ousting the Catholic hierarchy, and who saw to it that a secret committee should frame the new religion, at the head of which he put as Archbishop, an old Cambridge friend, companion, and dependent of his, Parker.

His subtlety in gradually derailing England from her Catholic course was amazing. He found in these first years of his power a country the whole bulk of which was still entirely Catholic, in practice, daily habit and tradition. He could not challenge directly a force of that kind, but he undermined it; he played the card of national feeling; he relied upon Philip of Spain, the chief Catholic champion, to plead with the Pope that the new English Church was, after all, tolerable and that the schism might not be permanent.

Meanwhile he prevented any direct action on the part of the Pope in England and he prevented a Nuncio from landing. Though the first laws had been passed making the worship in all the parish churches that of the new Anglican Establishment, yet the authorities winked at a large amount of toleration, going slowly in order to do their work more thoroughly later on. Men would take Communion in the Anglican form, and later take it in the Catholic form from the hands of the same parish priest; and Cecil boasted that no man suffered on account of his religion, only for treason to the State.

Throughout his life he continued to play that card of national feeling as the strongest he had in his game against Rome. Meanwhile, though openly the ally of Spain and even dependent upon Spain for maintaining Elizabeth's insecure position, he was working underground to produce an ultimate rupture with Spain, and his genius was never better shown than when, on the pretext of protecting them from piracy and also of examining into the credentials of the bullion they had on board, he detained in English ports the Spanish ships which had taken refuge there from pirates, while on the way to carry the pay to the Spanish King's soldiers in the revolted Netherlands. Cecil had calculated that Spain dared not fight since she needed England, small and weak though England then was, as an ally against France. It was taking a big risk, for if Philip had then declared war Cecil's game would have been ruined; but Spain did not declare war, and friendship was openly maintained between the two Crowns, though from that moment Philip of Spain knew that Cecil was working against him.

The Spanish effort in the Netherlands was ham-strung by this cutting off of supplies; and meanwhile the principal leaders of the old Catholic nobility in England were goaded into rebellion. They rose in the tenth year of Cecil's power, and that was Cecil's opportunity which he had himself created. The Catholic rebellion was put down with ghastly ferocity—drowned in blood. And Cecil could henceforward make use of the plea that attachment to the universal religion of Christendom was treason in any subject of Elizabeth's.

The plots for the re-establishment of Catholicism, and therefore for the destruction of Elizabeth, Cecil watched, discovered, and nourished, under his extraordinarily efficient spy system, at the head of which was, as we have seen, his man Walsingham.

The most famous example of his ability in this line was his catching of John Hawkins, the pirate and slave dealer, the man who was the teacher of Drake and, with Drake, the best seaman of his time. Cecil found Hawkins negotiating secretly with the King of Spain; having so discovered him, Hawkins' life was in Cecil's hands and Cecil compelled him to act as an agent and to continue to pretend to be Philip's friend, and to continue his correspondence with Spain. In this way Cecil discovered all that Philip was doing.

Next he patronized Drake, always disavowing the piracies and murders of that buccaneer, apologizing to Spain for the outrages, and even sometimes giving restitution, but all the while supporting Drake underhand and allowing him a small percentage of his loot by way of pay. He sheltered Drake from the most obvious consequences of his crimes, particularly in the case of the odious murder of Doughty; for we know now, though it was long hidden, that it was Cecil who prevented the prosecution of Drake by the Doughty family when they clamoured for justice.

Meanwhile, of course, open persecution of the Catholic Faith in England could, on the pretext of the recent rebellion, be launched. The old nobility, at the head of which was the Duke of Norfolk, were humbled, and the young Duke himself—though an ardent Protestant—was lured into a position where Cecil, feigning the deepest friendship for him, could bring him to the scaffold—which he did. From that moment, 1572, Cecil was supreme. He was at the height of his great powers, a man just over fifty, and completely dominating the sickly and chafing Queen, in whose name he acted.

The persecution grew more intense, until it was what I have called it—a reign of terror. But all the time Cecil, working hard upon the natural patriotism of England and insisting that he was only preserving the integrity and independence of the realm, maintained that the shocking executions and universal system of suppression and secret police work were not religious in motive, but only political. He kept to his formula, "that no man suffered for religion, but only for treason."

He exactly judged the moment when the weakness of France, through the religious war which had broken out in that country, would permit him to defy Spain, and to emphasize the now thoroughly Protestant character of the English Government. By the prevention of any educational facilities on the Catholic side; by the putting of all offices, academic or of magistracy or of the executive, into the hands of his creatures, he began breeding up a whole generation of young Englishmen in whom a strong minority—gradually turning into a majority—were opposed to the Faith. Yet throughout the business he kept the average Englishman bewildered as to whether it were really a fight between Catholicism and its enemies, or only between England and her political opponents.

When he had already grown old, and had begun to introduce his second son Robert (whom he had carefully trained in statecraft and who was his father's equal in brains and energy) to the conduct of public affairs, came the test of the Armada. Had the Armada succeeded there would have been, of course, a great Catholic rising, which could not have failed to be successful. Elizabeth would without doubt have yielded to her natural inclination and followed the Catholic desires of her people; Cecil would have fled if he had been able, or had he not been able would have been killed. But the Armada failed, and with its failure Cecil's great experiment took root and was founded for good.

He was then a man of nearly seventy; not long afterwards he died. That second son of his, as astute as his father, was a dwarf and hunchback with an enormous head, inheriting from his father, and continuing, the excellent spy system which was the basis of their power. He completed the work. This Robert Cecil (who was later made Lord Salisbury) lived to see the tide turned. He may not have actually launched, but he certainly knew all about, and nursed, the Gunpowder Plot; and his triumph on that occasion settled the collapse of the Faith in England.

Henceforward those in sympathy with Catholicism in varying degrees (and ardent Catholics were already a minority) were divided among themselves. It was the better part of a lifetime since the Mass had been forbidden in England; the heroic efforts of the Jesuits to create a reaction had failed, and though in mere numbers those who opposed the Catholic Church were not a large majority, they gave the tone to the whole.

England between 1605 and 1612, when Robert Cecil died, already stood before the world as a Protestant power, the only considerable Protestant power in Europe; and all this was but the completion of William Cecil's work. He, more than any other man, had made it possible for the Dutch Provinces in the Netherlands to throw over their legitimate Spanish King, and, though a very large minority of the Dutch were still Catholic, the new power of Holland stood side by side with England as a Protestant centre. Thus was the great work which William Cecil had set out to do in England and Europe accomplished.

On this account the whole of that decisive period in English history should properly be called "The Reign of the Cecils." It was they who introduced James I (just as they had introduced Elizabeth) to the throne; it was they who guided and shepherded the nation into the new paths.

Such was William Cecil; one of the greatest and certainly one of the vilest of men that ever lived. His work has outlived him and his associates by many hundred years.

HENRY IV OF FRANCE

WITH THE opening of the seventeenth century the Reformation enters its second phase. Its first had been a universal struggle to determine whether the Faith should be retained by *all Europe* or lost by *all Europe*. The struggle had been accompanied in Spain by violent repressions, in the Germanies by local conflicts, compromises and conferences, in France by violent civil war.

In England the Faith had been worsted by the consistent pressure against it of government, and with the loss of England (and Scotland under English power) the chance of a complete victory for Catholicism was lost. It was lost by 1606.

Henceforward we have in all Europe a second phase more political and less religious than the first: a division of Europe into two parts: Catholic and Protestant, which gradually crystallized and became permanent.

France fell after its exhausting civil war on to the Catholic side: but not thoroughly. The weakened combatants had ended by a compromise.

Henry IV of France was the typical figure of the compromise. He is symbolic of the way in which the great religious struggle of the seventeenth century in Europe was going to end.

It had long looked as though (1) it would end either by the complete dislocation of Catholicism and its replacement by a mass of Protestant sects, the enthusiasm of which would soon die away and leave civilization in ruins; or as though (2) the Catholic reaction would set in and would save the situation completely, as though the States and Cities which had rebelled against religious unity and looted Church wealth were going to be reconquered by Catholicism, partly through missionary work but, more, through the victory of the Catholic Princes and populations in the religious wars.

But in point of fact neither of these solutions took place. The great struggle ended without a decision. Towards the middle of the seventeenth century—round about 1650—the two cultures, now firmly established each in its own region, were left each facing the other.

The Catholic culture failed to re-establish itself completely throughout Christendom; the Protestant culture did not spread itself as it had hoped throughout all Christendom.

The first symptom of what was going to happen took place in France, at the beginning of this last phase, that is a little before the year 1600, after the religious wars. The struggle between the old religion and its enemies had been going on for a whole lifetime and fierce fighting, civil wars, popular revolts, etc., connected with the quarrel had extended over fifty years.

The active Government of the French people had lain for many centuries in the hands of a royal family called "The Capetian House" from their founder, Hugh Capet, who was the first King of that dynasty in France. The French Monarchy had a strict rule of succession whereby the next male heir must take the throne upon the death of the last King. The French Crown could not be inherited by a woman or even through a woman. For some hundreds of years it had gone from father to son without a break; then the last King had no surviving son, only a daughter, and the same was true of his brother who succeeded, so that the next male heir was only a cousin. Though this cousin was of the Capetian House he had a special title of his own, Valois—and the Kings descended from this cousin were called "The House of Valois."

Now, just when the Reformation quarrel was at its height, just at the moment when Queen Mary was trying to restore Catholicism for good in England and the Emperor in Germany was doing all he could to keep the peace between two sides, it became clear that the Valois line was going to fail also. There was a succession of three sickly young men, none of whom had heirs or probably could have had heirs. The nearest male heir was a distant cousin, and to find a common ancestor between him and the reigning King one had to go back nearly three hundred years.

This distant cousin belonged to a junior branch of the Capetian House which had the title of Bourbon, from their lands in the centre of France. Anthony de Bourbon, the head of the family, at the time when these sickly Valois boys were successively occupying the French throne, happened also to be King of a little Basque district on the extreme boundaries of France, just beyond the southern frontier, called Navarre. Being the next heir, he declared in favour of the Protestant cause, and his young son, Henry, who was a fine soldierly young man, very different from his sickly Valois cousins, was brought up to be a Protestant.

Something like half the nobility of France had also joined the religious revolt, hoping like their fellows and contemporaries, the English squires, to make a good thing out of it by looting the Church land, as had been done in England, Scotland, Northern Germany and Switzerland. They, therefore, began attacks upon the regular Government of the Valois Kings, who stood for the old orthodoxy. These attacks, from skirmishes and plots against individual lives, developed into regular civil war, called in the history of France, "The Wars of Religion."

The French Protestant rebels were called "Huguenots," and this heir-presumptive to the throne—Anthony de Bourbon, King of Navarre—was the head of the faction. The most powerful man, however, among the Huguenots was one of the three wealthy Coligny brothers, known as "The Admiral," because he was Admiral of France; that is, supervising naval business and drawing his revenue from wreckage, prize-money, etc., while his opponent, the most powerful man of the Catholic side, was the Duc de Guise, of the house of Lorraine.

The Coligny faction had murdered a Guise, and the Guise, therefore, watched to destroy the power of Coligny and his Huguenot followers. The Crown, which was really run not by the succession of sickly boys but by their mother, Catherine de Medici, a woman of great energy and intelligence, was determined to be subject neither to the one faction nor the other—and the most dangerous one at the moment was that of the Huguenots under Coligny. If they were sufficiently successful in their rebellious war they might come to command the whole country, change its religion, and, of course, loot all the Church wealth and become (as the English squires became in their turn) more powerful than the Crown itself.

It happened that a great number of Huguenots had come up to Paris to assist at the wedding of young Henry Bourbon, son of the King of Navarre, to the sister of the reigning King, who was Catherine de Medici's daughter. Coligny, plotting actively, was in Paris also threatening the Crown. The Queen-Mother determined, therefore, to have him assassinated. The populace of Paris, already intensely exasperated against the Huguenots, who were chiefly powerful in the South of France, seized the opportunity, and this first attack on Coligny was the signal for a general rising of the whole people of Paris on a scale which no one had expected.

The people chased the Huguenot gentlemen out of their houses and murdered them in the street, where there was a massacre of them and their servants. In great public disturbances of this sort many of course fall who are little connected with the real issue; debtors take the opportunity of getting rid of their creditors, and jealous men of their rivals. It is not known how many were killed altogether, but the probable number of victims in Paris was two thousand, and there were risings in many other towns as well.

This violent outburst of popular feeling against the gentry who were fomenting civil war is known as the Massacre of St. Bartholomew, because it began on the Vigil of St. Bartholomew's Day and continued on the day itself (August 22–3, 1572).

It is probable that this date for attacking the Huguenots was chosen and did not come haphazard. The Huguenots had been guilty of a particularly treacherous murder of Catholics on this same day, St. Bartholomew's Day, three years before; and it is said that the Royal family had sworn to have their revenge. Anyhow, it is generally known in history as "The St. Bartholomew."

The young Henry of Bourbon saved his life with difficulty. The massacre had a double effect. It exasperated the religious wars, of course, adding a powerful motive of vengeance to the original motive of religious difference—which was mainly avarice on the part of the Huguenot nobility; but it also had the effect of frightening the Huguenot faction, who had not guessed how violent the popular anger against them was. It showed that the temper of Paris, which counted for so much in those days in French affairs, was now definitely turned against the Reformation, and that the capital would have none of it; regarding those who supported it as traitors and rebels and public thieves.

The religious wars went on with great violence. Old Anthony de Bourbon, the King of Navarre, died and his son Henry succeeded him, but continued to lead the Huguenot forces in the civil war. The last of the Valois brothers was now King, under the title Henry III. His health was bad, he could certainly have no children, and he recognized Henry of Bourbon the new King of Navarre, who was his cousin, as his heir. But Paris was so angry with the Protestant faction (and so for that matter was the greater part of the country) that it refused to accept Henry of Navarre as its future King. It even preferred to break with the immemorial tradition of having the male head of the Capetian House for the Monarch, and prepared to put a younger heir upon the throne.

The principle of strict hereditary monarchy in the male line was so strong in France at the time that this seemed a desperate resolve. The King, Henry III, left his capital and took refuge with his cousin, Henry of Navarre, and together they besieged Paris from outside. A private man who was particularly excited against the Huguenot faction asked for an interview with the King, was granted it, and used the opportunity to stab Henry III to death.

With the death of the last Valois, Henry of Navarre was legitimate King of France. He had the powerful Huguenot army at his service and, because he had hereditary right on his side, though still a Protestant, numbers of the Catholic gentry joined him as well. The action of Paris in preferring religion to hereditary right was odious to them; but Paris held out and formed the centre of resistance to the Bourbon.

Up to this point it had seemed probable that Henry of Navarre would make good his right to the succession, and that France would have a Protestant King. If that should take place all the Protestant leaders (who were quite half the nobility of the country) would have received a great accession of power; a general loot of Church lands would certainly have begun after the pattern of what had happened in England, and probably the Faith would ultimately have been lost to France. Had France gone Protestant, the centre of gravity in Europe, from being with the Catholic culture, would have passed to the Protestant culture.

What saved the situation was the continued tenacity of the people of Paris. Although Henry of Navarre was still victorious they were determined not to give way; and, though they were subjected to a most horrible famine, they refused to yield.

At last it was Henry of Navarre himself who gave way. He may or may not have used the famous words, "Paris is worth the Mass!" but these words certainly expressed his sentiments. He himself, like most of his rank in those days, had no real religion. The Huguenot preachers, whom he had to listen to, bored him intensely; he was a very loose liver, much attached to his pleasures; the very opposite of a Puritan. He had the virtues of a soldier with no real faith in any doctrine. He judged that it would be better, after all, to accept the religion of the bulk of his subjects as, unless he did so, he might never be allowed to reign in peace.

This decision of Henry of Navarre to become Catholic was, as I have said, the first act of the great compromise by which Europe ultimately settled down into two opposing cultures—Catholic and Protestant. It marked the victory of popular Catholicism in France and the end of the chances—which once had stood so high—of Protestantism capturing that country.

But the thing was not a Catholic victory by any means; it was what I have called it, a compromise. Henry's old comrades in arms retained their violent opposition to Catholicism; his right hand man, Sully, who worked his finances and was even more avaricious than most of the Huguenot set, was an example in point; and on all sides the Huguenots retained great political power.

The new King further favoured them (with the object of retaining their support and reigning peaceably) by issuing an Edict known to history as the "Edict of Nantes." Under this arrangement a very large measure of toleration and something a good deal more than toleration was granted to the Huguenots. They were to be allowed to hold a certain number of strong towns and to garrison them and govern them independently, and thus form a sort of kingdom within the kingdom.

So, while in England Catholics were persecuted to the death—though still some half of the population—in France the Protestants—though but a small minority outside the noble class—were given all these advantages. They could practise their religion, of course, but, what was much more important politically, they could and did hold these strong places independently, whence they could make war against the Crown and threaten the mass of their fellow-citizens. They had, in particular, among these strong towns that of La Rochelle, an important seaport on the Bay of Biscay, which was as though in England at that time (it was towards the end of the reign of Elizabeth) the Catholics had been allowed to hold Portsmouth and, say, Chester, York, Leicester and a number of other walled towns in the kingdom.

So stood the compromise when Henry IV in his turn was stabbed, by another half-witted and fanatical defender of the Catholic cause who (quite rightly) doubted the King's sincerity. Henry IV, the first Bourbon King, died thus in the year 1610.

France was not, at his death, a fully Catholic country: on the contrary, it had become, through his action, a country in which a powerful anti-Catholic faction, counting many of the richest families in the kingdom, was tolerated and held important strongholds, as well as having the right to combine and put up effective resistance to the mass of the nation.

The ultimate result of thus establishing a dualism of religion was a current of French opinion which in the course of two more generations began to shift from Protestantism to a sceptical form of anti-Catholicism. But still, take it for all in all, the Catholic culture of France had been saved by Henry of Bourbon's abjuration. And that King, known to history as "Henri Quatre" had, though not intending to do so, saved the civilization of the country and of Europe—though hardly.

While this was going on in France, Henry's contemporary in England,

James I, was giving an example of a different kind. He was establishing the Protestant doctrine of the Divine Right of Kings, which has become, in course of time, the modern doctrine of the supremacy of the State over the Church and civil power over the religious power. How James I represented this, I will explain in the next chapter.

JAMES I OF ENGLAND

JAMES I of England struck at the beginning of the seventeenth century the note which was henceforward to affect all modern life so profoundly. That note was the independence of nations—as lay societies—from the moral judgment of the Church. Henry IV of France, his contemporary, was the symbol (as we saw in the last chapter) of the fact that the Reformation would not be successful in its attempt to overwhelm our civilization. In France, after a furious struggle in which the leaders of the nation had half of them gone Protestant and engaged in fierce civil wars against the other half, the nation as a whole had come down on the right side of the hedge, mainly through the energy of the city of Paris. But in France also the new nationalist spirit was rising, and we shall see later what a height it reached under Louis XIV, Henry IV's grandson, before the end of the century.

James I of England stands for that nationalist principle which, in the succeeding three hundred years, completely conquered.

To-day, everyone, for the moment, accepts the principle that the nation is sovereign and lay, completely independent of every international control. The modern nation gives no obedience to any defined international moral authority—such as had been the Catholic Church with the Papacy for its supreme Judge during all the centuries when our European civilization was being built up. The modern nation is not only completely independent, but admits no religious definition. Any citizen who prefers his allegiance to a religious body to his allegiance to the nation is regarded as a traitor. Religions of all kinds are regarded as the private affair of individuals. When the citizens differ among themselves upon religion it is the duty of the State to keep the peace between them but not to affirm itself the guardian of any one set of doctrines. The sacred thing to which everybody must adhere, the one doctrine against which no one may protest on pain of heresy, is the doctrine of patriotism and the right of the nation to its complete independence. There is, thus, no common law binding all nations.

Such, undoubtedly, is the present situation of the white world, Europe and the extension of Europe on the American Continent and in the various European Colonies and Dominions. How long this absolute nationalism will endure no one can say; one can only be certain that it will not last indefinitely. Of its nature it creates a state of affairs in which no nation—if it is strong enough to commit the crime—can be restrained from murdering another nation. There is no international police. Therefore, we have a state of affairs which is that of moral anarchy, mutually destructive, and—if it be pressed to its full conclusion—the absolutely certain end of our civilization.

Nationalism then, is, for the moment, enthroned; and James I at the beginning of the seventeenth century, when the great boiling mass of the religious quarrel was beginning to crystallize into nations Protestant and Catholic, inaugurated the full practice of nationalism.

Here it may be objected that the launching of this new doctrine (the first name of which was "The Divine Right of Kings") and the attempt to practise it was much older. For we must always remember that whether it is called "The Divine Right of Kings" or "The Full Independence of the Nation" it comes, as we shall see in a moment, to exactly the same thing, expressing the same idea and having the same consequences.

The first official and public statement of this sort was made by Cranmer, the first Protestant Archbishop of Canterbury, at the coronation of little Edward VI, as early as 1547; fifty-six years before James I came to the English throne. The doctrine had been formally enunciated in a loud voice from the altar steps of Westminster Abbey, in the sermon which Cranmer addressed to the little boy-King on his enthronement. Cranmer reminded him that no power on earth could claim any rights over the King of England, and he said this, of course, as a direct challenge to the Papacy.

Hitherto, it had been admitted throughout Christendom that quarrels between Christian nations were subject to the general moral authority of the Church, and to ultimate appeal to the Papacy in cases of specific dispute. In other words, Christendom had been regarded as one realm, of which the particular nations were only provinces; and a certain moral law and a certain visible organization were accepted as having common authority throughout. All the time between Cranmer's declaration and the accession of James I the matter had remained in dispute. To one group of men throughout Europe—and much the larger group—the new doctrine appeared monstrous and revolutionary; by another serious, though much smaller, group it was clung to desperately and advanced upon every possible occasion. We all know how furiously the battle raged in England itself and how, as late as twenty-four years after Cranmer's declaration, the Pope still claimed to release the *de facto* subjects of Queen Elizabeth from their allegiance *de jure* when he excommunicated that monarch.

The point about James I is not that he began the thing, but that he inaugurated its full and undisputed practice. At the end of that generation, not quite fifty years later, it was accepted everywhere that the religion of a State must follow the religion of its government.

At this point it is important to understand how this phrase, which sounds to us so quaint, "The Divine Right of Kings," is really identical with our most modern nationalist doctrine. In the time of James I, rather more than three hundred years ago, men talked of the thing in terms of the rights of Princes, that is monarchs, rather than in terms of the rights of nations. But it applied even then just as much to states in which there was no Prince; it applied to an independent democratic Republic like Geneva, or an aristocratic Republic like Berne or Holland, or to any one of the Free Cities of Germany, whether these were governed by a few rich men or by public opinion. The operative word in the sentence is not "King" but "Divine"—and when people talked of "Divine Right" they meant the right to govern with private responsibility to God alone, and not to any general organization of Christendom here on earth.

James I himself made this perfectly clear in the speech which immediately followed his coronation. He claimed the right to call himself "Catholic." The Church of England, of which he was now the head, uses that term in her formulae and recites it of course in the fundamental Creed generally called that of Nicea. James underlined this point with all his might, intending by this emphasis to reconcile with his complete sovereignty, if it were possible, that half of his English subjects, that minority of his Scottish subjects, and that overwhelming majority of his Irish subjects, who were fully Catholic in tradition—practising when they could or, when they could not, demanding the Mass and the full functioning of the old religion.

James did not at first desire to persecute that religion as William Cecil had done in the name of Elizabeth. What he did want was to get everyone to take the Oath of Allegiance which declared him to be the completely independent head of everything within his realm, clerical and lay. Therefore did he denounce with the utmost violence the claims of the Papacy and directed all his policy against them. He called the Pope "The Three-Headed Beast," so that there should be no doubt about his attitude; he reiterated the claim that the Crown of Great Britain was "Imperial," that is, subject to no other lay state, and he concluded that it was not subject to any external moral authority either.

It is interesting to note that James was, at one moment of his reign, in active negotiation with Rome (or rather with the agents of Rome) to see whether some formula could not be drawn up which would get over the difficulty of the Oath of Allegiance. If some set of words could be found which would satisfy the abstract Papal claim to depose a monarch by relieving his subjects of their Oath of Allegiance, some form of words making quite clear that acceptation by all subjects, clerical and lay, of the full sovereignty of the monarchy and its freedom from any kind of superior international power, he would have been content. No such formula was found; but it is significant that he should have made such efforts to discover one after his violently open break with Rome.

Many people think of James I as a man steeped in Calvinism, because he had been brought up under the rules of the Scottish Kirk. This is a great error. He had indeed been brought up in the main under the rules of the Scottish Kirk, but during the earlier years of life, when character is formed, there was a struggle as to whether that religious organization or its opponents should get hold of him. His own mother, Mary Queen of Scots, had died because she was strongly Catholic and because she represented the Catholic cause; and James himself always had a personal leaning, if not to the Catholic spirit, at least to Catholic individuals. His opposition to the Church was political rather than doctrinal; he prided himself on his learning, especially in theology; and it is only fair to admit that he did not pride himself without some cause. He was a very widely-read man, and one of high culture, though of displeasing and probably vicious character. He regarded pretty well any tenet as debatable, save that one tenet which roused him to wrath—the supremacy of the Pope in moral matters, even over sovereign Princes.

It is impossible to say what would have happened in the way of Catholic toleration under James I, but for the action of that man of genius, Robert Cecil. He was the second of the Cecils who governed England. His father, William Cecil, had taken over the management of the country in 1559, trained his son Robert to statecraft, and was succeeded by that son, without a break, although efforts were made in the transition of power from father to son to disrupt the succession by the introduction of new favourites. It was Robert Cecil, controlling the Government at the end of Elizabeth's reign, who had brought James to the throne, for the succession to Elizabeth was disputed, and the Queen herself had named nobody.

James came into England from Scotland with little knowledge of English ways, he talked with so strong a Scottish accent that it was not easy to understand him, and he brought with him a group of Scottish companions highly unpopular in England. It must be remembered that Scotland had been the hereditary enemy of England for centuries, and was still regarded as an alien nation. James depended more and more upon this statesman, Robert Cecil, who not only had the very highest talents as a statesman but was privy to all the secrets of the governing class around the King. He held firmly in hand a universal spy system and was adept, as his father had been, not only at discovering plots against the Crown, but at creating them by the use of secret agents and at nursing and fomenting them when they had started.

Now it was Robert Cecil's prime object to prevent a Catholic reaction. The whole policy of his family and tradition was the gradual imposition, by force and trickery, of the new religion upon the English people. They had so far succeeded that, when James thus came to the throne in 1603, quite half the English were opposed to their ancient Faith. Most of that half were, no doubt, indifferent to religion, as were many on the other side also; but in 1603 quite half England was, upon the whole, anti-Catholic; and it was Robert Cecil's business to make all England anti-Catholic in time; or, at any rate, if that should be impossible, to make so large a proportion of England anti-Catholic as to render the full return of the Faith out of the question. Whether he invented the Gunpowder Plot or not will always be disputed. There is no positive proof that he did; all that we know for certain is that he knew all about it just after it was started, and nursed it carefully. Gunpowder was then a Government monopoly, and yet the conspirators brought it openly across the Thames in large quantities, and all their movements were known. Cecil exposed the plot just at the right moment to produce the most effect; and it is from that date (1606) that the tide turns and that England tends to become more and more a Protestant country.

Cecil himself died rather early in James' reign, only half a dozen years after the great sensation of the Gunpowder Plot and the execution of the victims. But by that time his work was done. Catholics were hopelessly divided in England and no longer the bulk of the nation.

Meanwhile James, for the nearly twelve years in which he still had to live, hankered after Toleration. What he wanted was not only a quiet realm but a peacefully united one. He married his daughter to the very foolish Calvinist German Elector Palatine, who tried to usurp the Kingdom of

Bohemia and fell into disaster thereby; but he did everything to marry his only surviving son, Charles, to one of the great Catholic reigning families. He failed to make the match with Spain, but succeeded in arranging one with the Royal House of France. In the marriage treaty it was stipulated that Catholics in England should be free to practise their religion. He did what he could to prevent the butchery of priests, and, altogether, he was the originator of that Stuart policy of attempting religious truce which is one of the chief accusations against that dynasty raised against them by later official historians. He, and his son after him, and both his grandsons, Charles I and James II, all worked for toleration; not because they regarded religious toleration as a good thing in itself, but because they thought it good policy for the realm.

However, above everything else in the eyes of James I, the complete independence of the English Crown must be preserved. And it could only be preserved by supporting and continuing the Protestant policy of his predecessors. He stood for Divine Right. He watered and nourished that plant until it took firm root, and since his day has spread its doctrines everywhere, so that to-day (under another name) it is quite undisputed—with the consequences which we see around us.

FERDINAND II

THE EMPEROR Ferdinand II represents in the great religious struggle of the seventeenth century the strength of the Catholic reaction; that is, what is generally called the Counter Reformation.

If he had only represented that, however, his partial success and partial failure would be less interesting than they are. He also represents another feature which had come into the struggle and strongly affected it everywhere—*Nationalism.*

Everywhere in Christendom the particular interests of princes, cities, districts, nations and even of races or groups of culture, were at issue with the general interests of united Christendom. One main aspect of the Reformation, therefore, is the effort of the religious revolutionaries to assert local independence politically against authorities superior to themselves, and ultimately of course against the supreme moral authority of the Church throughout Europe.

It is convenient to call this force Nationalism because it was at its strongest where men's affection for their nation and their consequent desire for its complete independence was at work. But it was the same force even when there was no nation concerned. It was the force which, for instance, had armed the Slavs of Bohemia against the great German land-owners, the German dynasty which ruled them, the Empire of which they formed a part. That had been the principal meaning of the Hussite heresy and the wars which followed it in the century before Luther. In England, national feeling had also grown strong more than a hundred years before the Reformation. It had been emphasized by the new use all over England of the English language. Until a hundred years before the Reformation the governing class in England was still speaking French and this helped the cosmopolitan international feeling, and therefore attachment to the Church's authority. Even until some years after the date 1400, for half a life-time after Chaucer had begun to write, the most prominent men in England were still thinking, writing, and talking in French; for instance, William of

Wykeham, the great Founder of New College at Oxford, though born in a small Hampshire town, hardly more than a village, and not a rich man, was French-speaking. But by the time of Joan of Arc, say round about 1430, English had become universal in all classes. The upper class no longer thought or spoke in French, and this powerfully added to the unity and the common feeling of the nation.

Something of the same kind—a growth of separate national feeling—was going on in Spain, although there were several kingdoms there which only coalesced just before the Reformation took place.

The same thing had happened in France; strong united national feeling being apparent in that country at much the same time as it arose in England, though it was not quite so centralized, or so simple, or so coherent, as it was in England.

Now in the case of the German Emperor and his Empire, with their widespread and diverse territories, you could hardly talk of Nationalism, but there was this strong particular feeling for the hereditary power of a particular family, the ancient liberties of the free cities, the independence in as large a measure as possible of everyone with territorial power, from the small village Lord up to the Duke or Count of a whole province.

Ferdinand II is a character who, after a hundred years of religious division among Germans, undertakes to re-establish Catholicism everywhere in his dominions from the Alps to the Baltic, and from beyond the Rhine to the frontiers of Poland. He is the character who undertakes, as head of the German states, Emperor over them all, and individually the possessor of the largest amount of land as a private prince, to undo what the Reformation had done in nearly the whole of north Germany, and partly in the centre of Germany.

Had Ferdinand II triumphed the old religion would probably have been re-established not only in Germany, but, sooner or later, in most of Europe. Nothing would have remained of the religious revolution save the small populations of Scandinavia, of England and of Scotland, and no one can say how long these remnants could have stayed out; for there was a considerable Catholic minority in Scotland and in Scandinavia, and a very large one in England, as late as the beginning of Ferdinand's effort, that is from 1620–30. Even if England, Scotland and Scandinavia had remained strongly independent Protestant Governments, they would have counted little compared with the vastly greater numbers and wealth of the German Empire, France, Spain, Italy, Hungary, and Poland. The Protestants all put together would not have commanded one tenth of the men and money commanded by the Catholics, had Ferdinand succeeded in establishing a United Catholic German Empire.

But in his effort to restore Catholicism universally, on the Continent at least, Ferdinand II was also considering the power of his hereditary house, the house of Hapsburg; and it was this duality of aim which was at bottom the cause of his partial failure.

He succeeded to a great extent. To this day half the people who speak German are more or less Catholic; but he failed to sweep them all in. He had to end with a compromise which was completed after his death, and which from ten to eleven years after that date, left Germany permanently divided into two camps—Catholic and Protestant—which have never since joined.

The reason he failed was that the French, under their great Minister Richelieu, so feared an increase in the power of the House of Austria and the family of Hapsburg that though they were as a nation strongly opposed to the Reformation, and though they were led by a Priest and Cardinal, a great Churchman, yet he and the nation which he governed were the means to the preventing the Catholic success of Ferdinand.

The French under Richelieu were not only frightened of Ferdinand II's success, but of the corresponding success of the other branch of the Hapsburgs, the kings of Spain. The great Emperor of the Reformation time, Charles V, had divided his immense dominions, which one may say covered practically the whole of western continental Europe, except France, and all the Colonies of the New World except Brazil. He, as head of the Hapsburg House, had, on his resignation, handed over to his brother the German Emperor the hereditary lands of the Hapsburgs themselves within that Empire, the title, and, such as it was, the power attached to the Empire with its seat at Vienna. But he put his son's family over Spain, the Netherlands (which to-day we call Holland and Belgium), the country of the Jura, certain Italian possessions, and, of course, all the new colonies on the American side of the Atlantic. The Spanish Empire, governed from Madrid, and the European Empire, governed from Vienna, were in the hands of two closely related branches of the House of Hapsburg for much more than a hundred years. The Spanish Power helped the Emperor Ferdinand far more than if it had been a mere ally. They helped him with the whole strength of their Crown, regarding his cause as their own. This meant that the triumph of the Hapsburg at Vienna would also have been the triumph of the Hapsburg at Madrid. The whole western world would have fallen under the Hapsburgs, for France was the only considerable independent continental power, and it was encircled by Hapsburg territory upon every side.

What to-day we call Belgium was in the hands of the Spanish House of Hapsburg. The Empire covered Luxemburg and Alsace, and the Jura mountains. The same Spanish power lay everywhere south of the Pyrenees. There was only a short frontier of the Alps where an independent Italian Principality made an exception, and a very short distance on from the Alps, Spanish and Hapsburg power began again in the northern Italian plains.

It was on this account that Ferdinand's effort to restore Catholicism and undo the work of the Reformation lost its simple character and became complicated not only with the national desire of the French especially, but of many smaller powers as well, to retain their independence against the Hapsburgs.

In spite of this complication, however, which ultimately mutilated Ferdinand's plan and left him and his successors only half victorious, his chances of victory were considerable. When he began his effort, in the year 1619, it was almost exactly a hundred years after the Reformation had first broken out in his own Germany.

His chances of success were moral rather than material. They consisted in the very widespread and increasingly popular reaction towards the old religion. In the first heat of a great religious quarrel, say from 1520 to about 1560, the rebellion against the old organization of society, including the religious authority of the Pope and the immemorial Catholic Liturgy, was fiercely and increasingly successful. Those of the strongest temper and greatest initiative were on that side, and there came to their aid a very powerful incentive—the opportunity of looting the wealth of the old Church, which was enormous. But when the fury had spent itself, and when the main part of the looting had been accomplished, people woke up to the fact that what had been apparently no more than a generally confused and violent protest against corruption might well break up our civilization, and would certainly destroy the religion upon which that civilization was founded.

Instinctively, therefore, the populace everywhere was beginning to move, in the last half of the sixteenth century, in reaction against the hitherto successful religious revolt. The movement was powerfully aided by the establishment of the Jesuits, with their discipline and their complete singleness of aim—the most powerful factor in any moral effort. They sacrificed everything and they devoted everything to the restoration of religion, and within a lifetime they were educating the governing classes and the princes

on all sides, recapturing whole districts by preaching and example and organized effort. Side by side with this went a great Franciscan effort in the
same direction. This, and the success of the French Crown and the French
people in preventing Calvinism from sweeping France, started the advance
of the Counter Reformation, and the strong personality of more than one
Pope, especially of St. Sixtus V, aided in the general success.

Though the Counter Reformation was in full swing and seemed likely to
recapture morally all the ground that had been lost to Catholicism by the
Protestant movement, the various German states which were nominally
under the Emperor and which counted actually as part of the Empire,
lived under a compromise. The seizure of Church lands and wealth by the
Protestant princes, cities and local Lords, was tolerated, and there was no
serious, or, at any rate, no successful, repression of Protestant Government
in the regions controlled by these rebellious powers.

When Ferdinand became Emperor, already past his fortieth year, he
determined to put an end to this long-drawn-out compromise. He demanded the restitution of the looted wealth of the Church; not indeed of
the whole of it, but so much as had been irregularly seized after the solemn
engagements made in the middle of the sixteenth century, wherein those
who began the looting promised they would go no further than they had
already gone. Ferdinand demanded that what they had taken since that
date, in defiance of the pact, should be handed back again to the support
of religion.

It was always this financial demand, wherever it was made, which started the trouble. Exactly the same thing a few years later took place in Britain, when Charles I, on a much smaller scale, tried to get back some of
the looted wealth of the Church in Scotland. That was the real root of the
armed resistance which Charles had to meet and which ended in his defeat,
and death on the scaffold. It was Ferdinand's demand for restitution on a
much larger scale in Germany which led to the armed conflict there.

The particular event which started the main trouble was the quarrel over
the government of Bohemia. The kingdom of Bohemia belonged by hereditary right to Ferdinand, and he had been accepted as King of Bohemia
according to that right before he had become Emperor; but certain of the
magnates in Bohemia, notably Thurn (whose action in his country was
exactly like the action of Orange in Holland), determined to rebel. They,
or at any rate those who followed them, were not only moved by the fear
of losing the wealth they had seized from the Catholic Church, but also by
Slav feeling against the Germans, by national Bohemian feeling as well, and

in some degree by the Protestant enthusiasm of a minority. They declared that the kingship of Bohemia was not hereditary but elective. They threw Ferdinand's representatives out of the window from the Council Chamber in Prague, and they invited the only Calvinist prince in Germany, who governed the Palatinate (that is, roughly, the region north of Alsace along the Rhine), to come into Bohemia and be called King, ousting the power of the legitimate King Ferdinand. This young Elector Palatine was a very foolish, vain man, unfitted for the almost impossible task to which he had been summoned. Yet he thought he could bring it off because he had the strength of the English Government behind him (being the son-in-law of James I), and the sympathy of most of the German Protestants, and of course those elements in Bohemia which I spoke of: partly national, partly religious, partly financial. He went to Prague and was crowned King there, but Ferdinand easily re-asserted his rights. Within a year the Elector Palatine was not only driven out of Bohemia, but Ferdinand declared his own hereditary lands of the Palatinate confiscated for treason. The Catholic Ruler of Bavaria closely acted with Ferdinand to secure this victory, and was rewarded by being given the Palatinate for his share, to be added to his hereditary Bavarian lands. The Spaniards also came in to help, and it soon looked as though the struggle would be easily decided in favour of the new Imperial scheme. Ferdinand had been challenged in the wrong way. His enemies had given him the best opportunities for success. Many of the Protestant German princes hesitated to continue the struggle against their Emperor. The rebellious cities were on the whole more determined, and chief of them the very important city of Magdeburg, controlling the chief bridge across the Elbe in its lower part, where it forms the greatest military obstacle to any movement from the south against the north of Germany.

The Imperial arms in the war that was now being waged were superior to their opponents: in what way I shall describe later. They were almost certain to have won but for the fact that at the critical moment, about a dozen years after Ferdinand had come to the throne, Richelieu, alarmed by the approaching triumph of the House of Hapsburg in both its branches, had the perspicacity to hire one who he had been told was a man of military genius. This man was the young Swedish King Gustavus Adolphus, who had already engaged in hostilities on German soil upon the Protestant side. He was actually attacking his own cousin, the King of Poland—under conditions which I shall describe later on—when Richelieu approached him, and by raising his terms was ultimately able to buy the man's military genius, which he had appreciated with sure judgment. Richelieu did not himself declare war against the Hapsburgs. He launched Gustavus Adolphus against them, and though that genius was only in the field against Ferdinand for a twelve-month his action in that brief time almost overset the Catholic cause, and did in fact in the long run prevent its full success.

Ferdinand after that check lived on another half-a-dozen years, showing the utmost tenacity under disaster, meeting the most difficult and complicated circumstances of treason and further rebellion, and more or less restoring his own power, but not achieving what he had aimed at when he set out on the re-Catholicising of Germany. He was compelled to give way on the capital point of the restitution of Church goods. That of course was fatal. He began the struggle, as we have seen, in 1619. He kept it up for nearly twenty years until his death came in 1637. It was carried on after his death for another decade before it ended in exhaustion, with the two sides standing more or less as they had stood when the attempt began. The date 1648 may be taken as the final moment after which there could be no question of Germany's being united again either in one Protestant or in one Catholic state.

If any man could have succeeded it would have been Ferdinand, for not only had he the highest courage and the fullest tenacity of purpose but also the greatest devotion to religion and the finest personal character. He had, besides, what is of supreme value in governing men—sympathy with the masses and the humblest of his people. Anyone could approach him at any time. The population of his hereditary dominions was by the time of his death firmly bound to him with the bond of real affection.

But that fatal complication of Hapsburg ambition dreaded by France, and by all states and cities which it menaced, had come in to prevent the great experiment from succeeding. Nevertheless, Ferdinand when he came to die might say what most men say, who have attempted something perfect, failed to achieve it, yet partially succeeded. He could say like one of his descendants (Maria Theresa)—"There are no complete satisfactions." He had at any rate for the moment saved the Empire.

Richelieu and his Protestant allies accomplished their object in breaking the dominant power of the House of Hapsburg. By force of arms they had saved France from the fear of Ferdinand's rapidly growing influence. But they had dealt a shattering blow to the unity of the Catholic forces of Europe.

The resistance to Ferdinand had cost the German people a fearful price. This struggle, known in history as "The Thirty Years' War", dating from the first revolts in Prague, 1618, to the final peace in 1648, hugely impoverished the Germans, diminished their numbers to perhaps half of what they had been, left their commercial cities in ruins or crippled, and all hope of unity among them destroyed. From the time of its termination the Germans remained divided among themselves, and the French Power rose to its greatest height.

GUSTAVUS ADOLPHUS

WE SAW in discussing the Emperor Ferdinand II that his failure was mainly due to the discovery of a great military genius by Richelieu, the hiring of that genius by Richelieu in the interests of France, and the launching of him, also by Richelieu, against the Catholic Emperor.

The name of this genius was Gustavus Adolphus, King of Sweden. But for his quite exceptional talents in the art of war Ferdinand would have succeeded in making all Germans united under the Catholic Imperial Crown and in making Catholicism permanently dominating in Europe. The astonishing victories of Gustavus destroyed that opportunity, and Richelieu his paymaster was principally responsible.

Gustavus Adolphus was the immediate descendant of the man who had ousted the rightful King of Sweden from his throne. The Royal Family of Sweden was called Vasa. The Reformation in Sweden had followed the usual lines; the great nobles or landowners of that small country had looted the lands and other wealth of the Church, just as they did in England. They had been supported, as in England, by a small but enthusiastic minority of religious revolutionaries, and they had precariously established a Protestant government. The whole thing was done with more difficulty than in England because it came later. There were rich monastic establishments working almost to the end of the sixteenth century in Sweden, because, in spite of one small clique of men aiming to fill their own pockets, there was a succession of erratic monarchs, whose individual eccentricity prevented a continuous policy; for there was something of madness in all the Vasa family.

Now the legitimate heir to the kingdom of Sweden in the second generation of all this affair was strongly Catholic; and because he was hereditary King of Sweden, he was also the elected King of Poland—a country which, after much hesitation, had come down strongly on the Catholic side. This legitimate hereditary King of Sweden, Sigismund, thus became at one and the same time, the King of Sweden and of Poland. Even strong Protestants in Sweden hesitated to take the full step of rebellion and refuse to accept his sovereignty; for that would have been shocking to the ideas of the time. But, being determined to keep their Church loot and at the same time to maintain the independence of Sweden, so that her affairs should not be merged in those of Poland, they made the young King swear to respect all the institutions of Sweden and maintain the Reformation settlement of land in that country.

Such a situation was too unstable to last. The vested interests created by the loot of the Church in Sweden were, as in England, terrified lest a Catholic monarch should restore the Church's wealth to its rightful owners, and they repudiated, in spite of their oaths, their legitimate king and adopted for their candidate to the throne his usurping uncle.

When the usurping uncle, who thus held the throne of Sweden against all right, died, he left a young heir, by name Gustavus Adolphus, and that young heir was at once regarded by all those who had made their fortunes out of the religious revolution as their champion. For they did not know, what was soon to be proved, that he was not only the leader of anti-Catholic influence in his little country (a community not much larger than Scotland then was—at the most a million and a half souls) but a man unique in his time for the power of moulding and using an armed force. Young Gustavus Adolphus began by making the wealthy men of his country impress by forcible conscription as great a force as so small a community could yield. He then crossed the Baltic and launched out into adventures on German and Polish soil, to the south of that sea.

He was occupied in fighting his cousin, the Catholic King of Poland (upon whose throne he was himself a usurper), when his reputation reached the ears of the great French Prime Minister, Richelieu.

Richelieu had that quality which one continually finds throughout history in men who decide the course of international affairs successfully. He could foresee the results of character. It is true that Gustavus Adolphus had already given proofs of talent, but on a small scale and in a small field. Richelieu had gambled, if gambled be the right word, on the chance of Gustavus proving to be what, in fact, he did prove to be, a captain of the first rank. Richelieu sent an agent to approach Gustavus during his Polish war and to offer him money on a large scale if he would direct the attack on Ferdinand, who was in the midst of his hitherto successful experiment of recapturing Germany and establishing the power of the Emperor over the cities and smaller states. The first offer Richelieu made to Gustavus was high: three big tubs of gold. Gustavus (who is always represented to us as the champion of ideal causes) held out for five. Richelieu was determined to secure his services and therefore agreed to the five tubs of gold. When this had been settled—and not before—Gustavus was ready to march.

At first it looked as if the new situation would not make a very great change in the religious and political war among the German. Many of the German princes were jealous at seeing a Swede laying down a policy for them and enforcing it by his army. Some of them, though Protestant and northern, that is, far removed from Vienna, thought it was better policy to remain neutral. Moreover, they did not yet suspect (nor did Gustavus himself properly understand) what vast talent the Swedish king possessed in the trade of arms. This was soon to be manifest.

The Thirty Years' War between Ferdinand and the Protestants had been going on for more than ten years. The critical point, at the moment when Gustavus Adolphus entered the struggle, was with the town of Magdeburg, of which I have just spoken. It was the lowest main crossing of the obstacle formed by the river Elbe, which prevented the Emperor's armies working from the south to master the Baltic shore. Therefore, the Imperial forces of Ferdinand were besieging Magdeburg. It will always be doubtful whether Gustavus Adolphus might or might not have relieved the town, and whether his failure to do so was due to personal prudence (that is, his conclusion that the risk of attempting it would be too great), or to the stubborn neutrality of the Protestant German princes who stood between him and the city. At any rate he did not relieve it, and the rebel town upon which the eyes of all Protestant Europe had been attracted was stormed and sacked by the Imperial General Tilly and his army. The most horrible barbarities were committed, and nearly the whole place was burned down. Though Tilly did his best to restrain the soldiery he cannot be absolved from responsibility for the massacre which the rebels suffered.

Gustavus Adolphus published an open defence of his failure to relieve the town, upon the value of which defence opinion is divided to this day. At any rate, shortly afterwards, the striking Imperial successes had got him further Protestant alliances, and he began marching southward against the Imperial armies, side by side with his Protestant German allies. It was at Breitenfeld, in the plain of north Leipzig, on the edge of the hills that bound this plain, that Europe woke up to the King of Sweden's genius.

Then for the first time did Richelieu find himself amply justified in having hired him to reduce the power of the Hapsburgs. Indeed, Richelieu found that he had purchased service too strong for him and likely to embarrass his own plans. For Gustavus Adolphus, after his German Protestant allies had broken, restored the battle and not only defeated the army of the Imperialists under Tilly but virtually destroyed it. The remnant of the Imperialists fought magnificently for hours, but only a fraction could be led in formation off the field. All the baggage had gone and all the artillery. It looked at the moment as though this battle would make all Germany Protestant.

For exactly a year Gustavus Adolphus now gathered to himself greater and greater forces from all the rebel and Protestant elements in the Empire, and advanced southwards and westwards. He went to the Rhine. He held a sort of Imperial Court at Frankfurt. He very nearly did what Bismarck was to do more than two hundred years later—convert the German Empire from a Catholic to a Protestant power. The great powers of Europe paid him court as though he were already in possession of Imperial authority—all this in quite a few months after that tremendous victory near Leipzig.

As may be imagined, Richelieu was frightened by the unexpectedly great success of his hireling. He did what he could to save the Catholic cause in Germany and he got verbal promises from the victor, but he doubted their being kept. He was thoroughly alarmed at the too great measure of success he had obtained by his right judgment of the military talents of the Swede.

Gustavus Adolphus, having thus made himself supreme upon the Rhine and having swept over the whole of the north and centre of Germany, proposed to turn upon the hereditary lands of Ferdinand II and to strike at the heart of the old Imperial power. There was a moment in which it looked as if he might have seized Vienna itself. He crossed the Danube, he invaded Bavaria. The great Tilly died of wounds received in action, and it seemed as though the Catholic and Imperial cause were now really lost for ever in the Germanies.

At that moment, in desperation, Ferdinand called upon the captain who had formerly led the Imperial troops to victory, Wallenstein. It was a risk, for the army would follow Wallenstein in person rather than the Emperor, and no one knew what Wallenstein would do if he should prove successful again. He was quite unscrupulous and was playing his own hand. Armies in those days were nearly all mercenary. They followed a leader for pay and the Imperial Government was poor. But Wallenstein, thus recalled, held a name which worked miracles among his soldiers.

Ferdinand, then, took the risk and Wallenstein marched against Gustavus Adolphus, whose centre at the moment was Nordlingen, a nodal point in the communications between the Danube Valley and the north of Germany. Wallenstein refused to attack for a long time. He entrenched himself in the neighbourhood of Nordlingen until at last he provoked the King of Sweden to attack him, almost exactly a year after the first spectacular victory of the Swedes at Breitenfeld.

The shock came in 1632 on a day of fog and bewilderment. One may say that the Swedes had the best of it. Wallenstein lost his artillery and was tactically beaten; but there was no true decision, and the essential fact of the day was that Gustavus Adolphus happened to be killed in the turmoil. He probably fell through the accident of losing his way in the fog and getting surrounded by a detachment of enemies. At any rate the death of the great Protestant hero shook the whole fabric of his enormous, but ephemeral, success.

What followed was a series of ups and downs. The Swedish prestige could not be permanently maintained. The Imperial forces recaptured a sufficient ascendancy to dominate, more or less, their opponents, but not to dominate them completely. The Emperor, as we saw in the last chapter, was compelled, owing to the intrigues and surreptitious treasons of the time, to give up the essential of the whole affair—the restitution of Church goods.

Further, Ferdinand discovered that Wallenstein was likely to betray him. For the great but unscrupulous captain had all the strength now of an independent monarch, and Ferdinand was determined to reassert himself. His Spanish allies (that is the other branch of the Hapsburg House) furnished a new army and the Emperor behaved with admirable courage and tenacity during the crisis in which the more than suspected treason of Wallenstein threatened his throne and his life. Ferdinand had the strength of will and the judgment to dismiss that too dangerous nominal subject who was really his rival. Wallenstein then betrayed the Emperor and entered into communication with the Swedes, who were still the nucleus of the anti-Imperial forces. But the Emperor in this moment found men to serve him. Wallenstein was bearded in his quarters even in the moment of his betrayal and was put to death by a group of officers in the Imperial service. His second in command had already proclaimed his own loyalty to the Emperor.

With the death of Wallenstein the Emperor was free from his principal danger within, but lost his most talented commander. The struggle dragged on, lingering, until after Ferdinand's death. The Thirty Years' War did not end until the general pacification of the mid-century, in the treaties which are usually known as the Peace of Westphalia. These were signed just before the triumph of the English revolution against Charles I, and one may say that, after 1650, Europe was finally settled into the opposing cultures which it has since maintained. North Germany, thanks to the efforts of Gustavus Adolphus and in spite of his death eighteen years before; thanks also to the statesmanship of Richelieu, the paymaster of Gustavus Adolphus, who was also by this time dead—was to be securely Protestant and its princes and lords and cities to keep the loot of religion. Catholicism in South Germany was saved, nominally, and the power of the Emperor was still maintained; but it had failed to make a united country of its subjects. The great Swedish general had done his work well.

RICHELIEU

OF ALL the public characters who moulded Europe during the seventeenth century Richelieu is both the greatest in himself, and the most important in the effect he had. He perpetuated in France the presence of a Huguenot (that is a Protestant) minority among the wealthier classes, and he confirmed the independence of Protestant Germany, initiating the breakdown of Catholic authority represented by the Emperor at Vienna.

In other words, it was Richelieu's genius more than any other factor which led to the great battle ending in a draw, and to a Europe from one half of which the Catholic culture was to be permanently excluded.

Most people would still say, being asked what was Richelieu's lifework, "The Consolidation of the French nation through the strengthening of the French monarchy." That was certainly his intention; it was certainly the object to which he himself was devoted; everything else he did was subsidiary to that in his own mind. But the fruits of a man's work are never those which he expects—there is always some side effect which will seem after a certain lapse of time to be the principal one. A man wins a battle in order to obtain a crown and the result—unexpected by himself—is a change of language over a wide district. A man protects some oppressed people and liberates them from their oppressor and the result—unexpected to himself and coming perhaps a hundred years later—is the conquest of his own people by those whom he had befriended. A man raises a rebellion to establish democracy, and the result is government by a financial oligarchy.

So it was with Richelieu. The one thing he cared about was giving the French people political unity, which could only be done by making the King strong. He succeeded; but the result was to leave the French morally divided between Catholicism and its enemies; while the much larger indirect result which has affected the whole world was the creation of a firmly planted Protestant North Germany typified to-day by the power of Prussia, and all this power has meant during the last hundred and fifty years.

The way Richelieu set about his task of strengthening the French people was as follows:

He had noticed how during his own youth the great nobles and especially the great Protestant nobles were blackmailing and weakening the Crown, after the assassination of Henry IV. The worst culprit was old Sully, who went off with enormous loot as the fruit of threats to aid civil war against the Queen Regent. The King, the heir of Henry IV, was only a boy, under the title of Louis XIII; until he should be of age his mother, Marie de Medici, a violent but unpractical woman, was left in control. The result was that the rich could do pretty well what they liked. The Protestant nobles and the large Protestant middle class of the towns took full advantage of this position. It will be remembered that Henry IV, by the Edict of Nantes, had allowed them to hold a number of strong walled cities and to govern them as a sort of State within the State, and had also permitted them to call national assemblies of their faction, which were a perpetual menace to the central power of the King. Richelieu saw that the first thing to be done if the Crown was to be saved, its power increased and thereby the whole nation consolidated, was to take away these dangerous special favours, and treat the Huguenots like everybody else. He was determined when he came to power that there should no longer be a realm within the realm, and a rival power strong enough to threaten the monarchy.

But by so much as he was determined upon this was he also determined upon the fullest toleration for Calvinism. Richelieu was the first of that long line of public men from his day to ours to treat religious difference as a private matter, and to believe that one can have a united country without unity of religion. James I of England, as we have seen, had some such idea at the back of his head; but he never really put it into practice, for the hatred and fear of the Catholic Church of the great land-owners his subjects, whose fortunes had come from the loot of the Church, was too strong for him. And what is more, the great landowners proved in the long run too strong for the English Crown, and destroyed it, substituting their own two assemblies, the House of Commons and the House of Lords, known as "Parliament," for the old popular kingship of England. Richelieu saw the menace, though it had not fully developed in his own time, and he was determined that France should follow the opposite course. It is therefore due to him not only that France became politically united as a strong monarchy, but also that the peasantry won the long battle with the noble classes and became the main owners of the soil of France; whereas in England the noble classes, that is the squires, ate up the peasantry and became the main owners of the soil themselves.

Richelieu's most famous exploit in this reduction of the political power of the French Huguenots was the siege and capture of their strong town, the port of La Rochelle. To satisfy Protestant feeling in England the King of England, Charles I, had tried to succour the place by sending the Duke of Buckingham there with a fleet and an army. Buckingham very nearly succeeded, and would have quite succeeded—for he was an excellent soldier and laid his plans well, not attacking the town directly, which would have been a task beyond his powers, but threatening it in flank by seizing the great island at the mouth of the harbour—but having such an opponent as Richelieu to face, he lost. La Rochelle was captured for the King of France, and the Huguenot political privileges were at an end.

All the more was Calvinism tolerated as a religion. In that very lifetime which saw priests butchered in England after the cruel fashion for which the Puritans were openly responsible during their period of power, Calvinism in Catholic France was perfectly free. It had no martyrs and suffered no persecution. Although its followers were a minority among the French people they were a considerable proportion of the wealthy class, and it was from them that the anti-Catholic feeling among the French gradually developed. Their influence did not take the form of converting any further numbers to Calvinism, but of familiarising masses of Frenchmen with a dislike of the Catholic Church; so that at long last, after ferment had been at work for a couple of centuries, the whole nation was divided upon the issue—and remains violently so divided to this day. This religious division is the principal source of French weakness at the present time.

While Richelieu thus—without intending to do so—sowed the seeds of religious division in France he—also without intending to do so—sowed the seeds of that much graver growth, the religious division of Europe. We have seen in what was said in the chapter concerning Gustavus Adolphus, how the centre of Europe was being recaptured for the Faith. The government of the British Isles was Protestant, and a determining majority of the population of Great Britain was Protestant; but Ireland was Catholic and there was a large Catholic minority in England. In Holland, where there was a Calvinist Government, there was a still larger Catholic minority. It was only in Scandinavia that you had a Protestant population with no appreciable Catholic resistance remaining, and no one could guess as yet that one of these ill-populated countries—to wit Sweden—was going to produce a great military genius in Gustavus Adolphus. Long before Gustavus Adolphus appeared on the scene Richelieu had watched with anxiety the increase of Catholicism in Germany, and the recapture of district after district for the Faith. And he had watched what seems to us to-day so natural a matter for rejoicing in a Catholic statesman with anxiety, because he was thinking more of the power of his King than of the Faith. To do him justice he could not have conceived that Catholicism in Europe would ever be in serious danger.

The Protestant nations were small and divided and hardly seemed to him a menace. England had at the most a third and more probably not much more than a quarter of the population and wealth of France; Holland still less; the three Scandinavian countries—Norway, Denmark and Sweden— less even than Holland, for large as Sweden and Norway between them look on the map much the most of their territory consists of uninhabitable mountains. Further in the Germanies, Protestantism was represented by a number of separate states and small principalities, jealous of each other and able to offer no permanent resistance to the advancing power of the Catholic Emperor, who ruled from Vienna and was determined to make all Germany a united nation under his own rule.

But such a nation would have been a menace to France, and Richelieu set out to prevent such unity from being accomplished. Now that this military genius, Gustavus Adolphus, had appeared unexpectedly like a me- teor in the international world, he realized the opportunity, and we saw in the last article how he hired Gustavus to be his soldier against Austria. Gustavus was defeated and killed in the very nick of time for Richelieu: a little more, and he might have restored a united Germany of another sort. As it was, when he died he had saved Protestantism but had not extended its boundaries.

Richelieu, who had now become seriously alarmed at the unexpected magnitude of his prodigious success, felt free again—but even as it was the challenge which he had thrown down to Austria was very nearly the ruin of his plans. The huge Spanish Empire was governed by another branch of the same family as that which ruled the Catholic German Empire—the family who took their name from the Castle of Hapsburg. The Hapsburg ruling in Spain was the cousin of the Hapsburg ruling in Vienna. Part of the Spanish Empire in those days was the country now called Belgium. The Spaniards had far greater money resources than the French in the early seventeenth century, and though Spanish power was declining no one sus- pected how far that decline had gone—for it was from within. The external appearance was still magnificent. They came very near to a decisive and crushing victory over the French—but they failed. Richelieu maintained French power victoriously until his death, and the chief result of his policy was the falling in of Alsace under the French monarchy. The nobles and free cities in that wholly German-speaking plain lying between the Vosges and the Rhine were divided, about one-third being for the Protestant cause and about two-thirds for the Catholic. But no one there wanted to be under the Emperor; and one of Richelieu's Protestant allies, who was fighting the Emperor, having been killed just after he had captured Brisach, the key-fortress on which Alsace depended, his Army was persuaded to solve its difficulties by offering the Government of Alsace to the King of France. It was not a bad bargain for the Alsatians, all of whose local liberties remained, and who came nearer to enjoying self-government over the space of a century and a half than they were likely to come under either of the two rivals on the other side of the Rhine—the Emperor or his Protestant opponents.

Richelieu died in 1642, having seen all his schemes come to success. They came late. He could not be certain of his triumph until the very last years of his life. Even as his last sickness was upon him, when he was a dying man, it still looked as though the Spaniards in the South might be too strong for the French, although their attack from Belgium had been defeated. But by the actual moment of his death Richelieu knew that he had conquered everywhere. What he did not know (but what the Pope of the day foresaw rather vaguely) was that the triumph of the French Cardinal meant also the permanent establishment of Protestant power in Europe.

LAUD

LAUD WAS the Protestant Archbishop of Canterbury under Charles I of England. He belonged to that generation which was born somewhat before the year 1600 and which was old by the middle of the seventeenth century—that is, by the time that each party in the great religious quarrel of the Reformation was dimly appreciating that the battle was a drawn one, and that there could not be a complete victory on either side.

It will be remembered that the middle of the seventeenth century, and more particularly the date 1648 (The Treaties of Westphalia), marks that moment of exhaustion on the two sides. After it, what used to be united Christendom was permanently divided into the two camps of the Catholic and Protestant cultures, the boundaries of which have not appreciably changed from that day to this. Laud, as Archbishop of Canterbury, was the principal figure in English official Protestantism; that is, in the new establishment set up by William Cecil, and known as "The Church of England" in the critical period when the conflict was being decided. He was put to death by the English revolutionaries a little before the general settlement just mentioned; and he had begun his characteristic activities less than twenty years after the beginning of the century.

His personality is most interesting. He was of the middle ranks of society, with no special advantages of birth, and gained public attention wholly through his own energy and character. That energy was intense and never failed him to the end; it was as great in his last days as in his first and it animated a very small body—for he was almost a dwarf in size. His volume of work and correspondence was enormous, his power of attention to detail was equally great, and he followed a fixed clear policy with great chances of success, which was only defeated by the rise of a general rebellion against the English Royal Government, in which his own activities and office were included.

The importance of Laud in any study of the great religious quarrel and its unsatisfactory drawn settlement in the seventeenth century is considerable, and it lies in this: he was an early example of how the great Catholic recovery which had marked the end of the sixteenth century reacted upon the Protestant world. But at the same time Laud is a still more striking example of the way in which the Reformation had made the Protestant attitude of mind unescapable for those who had broken away from Catholic unity. In other words, the interest of his career lies in this—that in spite of certain sympathies with Catholic tradition and in spite of their recovering certain sides of the general European culture, the Protestants throughout Europe and even in England (where Catholicism was still so strong), were condemned to be the victims of the original violent rebellion which had taken place in their fathers' time.

In the case of Laud, and of England in general, this was particularly striking because the force which made against their returning to Catholic unity was the force of nationalism; that is, the claim of lay society and its Prince (or King) to independence from the general moral unity of Christendom and the West. All of this is summed up of course in the refusal to accept Papal Supremacy.

Laud was the chief and leader of those who had come to deplore the losses inflicted by the Reformation and the wounds which it had inflicted upon normal human habit. He was the leader and representative of those who feared and disliked Puritanism as a moral disease. He had sympathy with the natural and excellent use of images in worship. One of the counts in the indictment against him on which he was put to death was his having put up a statue of Our Lady and the Holy Child, which one may still see standing above the main door of the University Church of Oxford (St. Mary's). He and those like him, who were now becoming numerous in the English Established Protestant Church, not only felt a sentimental attraction towards the lovely and human externals of Catholic worship, but were also inclined—one cannot use a stronger word, but at any rate *inclined*—to consider the fullness of Catholic doctrine in nearly all points.

They inclined (as their descendants, the High Churchmen, do to-day) to an explanation of the mystery of the Eucharist more and more approximating to the truth. They inclined to Sacramental Penance and the Sacramental view of religion in general. They were particularly strong upon the necessity of a hierarchy and upon what they hoped was in their own case and what they admitted in the case of Catholics to be, the Apostolic Succession. They desired to regard their clergy as priests and some of them indeed would come to say even "sacrificing priests." But with all this they remained Protestant. They remained (though they would not have admitted it) thoroughly anti-Catholic, because they rejected that one part of Catholic doctrine which is its essential—the combination of unity and authority. The unity of the visible Church and its invincible authority were repugnant to their growing nationalism, and those who preserved such an attitude of mind were just as much the enemies of Catholicism as the most rabid Puritan could be, or the most complete agnostic.

Laud himself used a phrase which has become famous in this regard: he said that he could not consider reunion "with Rome as she now is." Now that phrase was not only a rejection of unity, but by its wording it implied that there was no united visible Church of God on earth. The use of the word "Rome" in this connection emphasized and was intended to emphasize the doctrine that "the Church of Rome hath erred "—which inevitably includes the doctrine that "all the Churches [as the phrase goes] had erred"; and that therefore there was no united visible infallible Church.

There is to be remarked, embarrassing Laud and his followers in this early stage of the Great Quarrel, just the same difficulty which embarrasses High-Churchmen or so-called "Anglo-Catholics" to-day. It is impossible for them to give a clear definition of their position, because they, while abhorring the word Protestant, are essentially Protestant in refusing unity and in preferring a national religion, which can include any degree of heresy, to an international religion which excludes all heresy.

If you were to have asked Laud what doctrines he taught, he would have replied with some, though insufficient, definition. If you had gone on to ask him, "Do you separate yourself from those within your national Church who deny these doctrines? Do you cut them off from their communion?" he would have had either to answer "No," or to remain silent. To those Protestants of his own day who were violent against other Catholic doctrines besides that of unity, who hated the doctrine of the Real Presence, who detested any sacramental system, who were excited to anger at the idea of a priesthood—in other words the Puritans—Laud and those who thought with him seemed to be half Catholic. They seemed to be leading England back to Catholicism. They were even spoken of as "Papists" by the more extreme of their opponents. But all that was false and an illusion. In certain externals they proposed to imitate or recover certain Catholic practices, and they did cherish an affection for much of the Catholic spirit, but that which is the very heart of the whole affair, "*ut sint unum,*" they rejected.

Nor did they reject it with reluctance; their rejection of it was fundamental to their whole position. It was a position expressed in many phrases, all of which strongly illuminate its character. Thus there is the phrase which speaks of the Church of England as "The Church of our Baptism"; there is the phrase which calls the Pope "an Italian Priest." (We were implored only the other day by a high dignitary of the Church of England "not to grovel at the feet of an Italian priest.")

Just as the rejection of unity coupled with infallible authority, is the intellectual or doctrinal test of Laud's Protestantism, so in that equally important matter of the emotions, and affection, is repugnance for the true Church in communion with the Pope as the centre of unity, the test of his Protestantism also. The Catholic Church of its nature excites either great loyalty or repulsion. When it excites repulsion in a man, that man is the enemy of the Faith, even though he accept the greater part of its doctrine and the greater part of its traditional externals, and an organization and discipline under a hierarchy similar in name to the Catholic.

Now for the Catholic Church Laud and his followers felt repulsion instead of affection. They felt (to use a modern phrase) that it was "un-English." In other words, their religion must be national, and the fact that a true and universal religion must necessarily be international was to them a strong irritant. It is this which explains the deep and permanent sympathy which existed between Laud and his King, Charles I, who had made him Archbishop. Charles had not the same sentiment of sympathy with many Catholic externals that Laud had; he was by temperament what we call to-day Evangelical. An experience of his very early youth—his voyage to Spain and the failure of his Royal marriage there—had emphasized his strong dislike of Catholicism. He sincerely believed that the Church of England, as he had known it with its ceremonies and ministers in his boyhood, was the most perfect Christian organization; and therefore his attitude implied that there could be many such organizations side by side, many Churches, and no one infallible authoritative Church.

Charles disliked the Mass in spite of his increasing affection for his Catholic wife, the sister of the King of France; he disliked the Catholic priesthood and their whole spirit; he had nothing about him of what we call to-day the High Anglican. Yet he got on capitally with Laud and Laud with him, the reason being that the real devotion of each was towards the Royal and national power, the complete independence of the English realm and the English King from all other authority, spiritual or temporal.

The effort at unity which Laud made had little to do with spiritual unity, even within his own communion. He was there concerned with unity of practice, with imposing a similar liturgy upon England, Scotland and Ireland. For the sake of dignity and for the sake of historical tradition Laud would see to it that the liturgy was interpreted in terms of considerable pomp and careful ritual, but he did not impose dogma.

He was determined that the English Communion should be the only Communion service wherever the King of England ruled, that it should be given at the altar rails and not haphazard at a table in the middle of the Church, that the Elements should be received kneeling—and so forth. But he was content to leave aside the essential definition of what the Real Presence was—whether or no Jesus Christ appeared on the altar at the consecrating words of a priest. These, which are to the Catholic mind the essentials, seemed to him things no doubt important, but not essential; the essential was the unity of the Church of England and its independence from the general Christendom of Europe.

The activities of Laud's life and the manner of his death have between them made him of considerable effect upon the subsequent history of the Anglican Church. His activities were political, strongly supporting the monarchical government which was then the traditional government of England—personal government by a King responsible to the nation, the centring of power in an individual whose duty it should be to defend the weak against the strong and prevent the wealthier classes from lording it over their fellows. On account of this political activity Laud was swept into the great revolutionary battle of his time.

The interests of the wealthy, the merchants and money-dealers of the City of London, the interest of the squires and the great land-owners—all these made for rebellion against the power of a personal King. In many the movement was hardly conscious, many hesitated to join the rebellion, very many went against their own class interest and defended the monarchy when it came to the actual issue of arms. Nevertheless what are called "The English Civil Wars" were essentially a struggle between wealth and the Crown.

Early in that struggle the interests of wealth allied themselves to, and were mixed with, the violent religious passions of Puritanism. A very large proportion of land-owners and a far larger proportion of the great merchants were Puritan. Therefore, as the struggle increased in violence Laud became the target for a double attack. He had repressed Puritanism in religion, he had supported personal monarchy in politics. His person was seized by the rebels, he was imprisoned, and at last they put him to death.

Such a career and such a termination to it created what may be called "The Legacy of Laud." Politically that legacy came to nothing. The victory of the wealthier classes in England was so complete and the corresponding defeat of the monarchy so thorough that the very idea of government by a King died out in about half a century after Laud's death. One long life-time after his beheading on Tower Hill the English throne was filled by a puppet monarch who was not even allowed to attend the governing Council of the realm. And from that day onwards England has been governed by the great land-owners and by the money-dealers of the City of London.

But the legacy of Laud in ecclesiastical matters had more vitality. It fell very low during the eighteenth century, but it was revived before the end of that century when a sermon—famous in its time—was preached from the pulpit of the University Church of Oxford in favour of Sacramental Absolution and the revival of the Sacrament of Penance in the Church of England.* There followed, in the same lifetime, the Tractarian Movement, and there now exists in greater force than has hitherto been known, a Laudian spirit acting in varying degrees throughout one great section of the English Protestant Establishment. The more devoted followers of that spirit go far beyond Laud himself in their imitation of Catholicism, and even in the attempt to recover the spirit of that from which they are separated; a considerable minority express themselves openly in favour of that reunion with the Catholic Church which Laud himself rejected.

Such is the Legacy of Laud. We must beware of being led by its present form from reading into his own life more than that life meant. He was in his own time distinctly and clearly anti-Catholic, wholly devoted to a separate English Church of which the special mark was refusal of communion with the Catholic Church as a whole and rejection of its authority. But he does show how the recovery of Catholicism after the first assaults of religious revolution affected one section of Protestantism in Europe.

As against this, within the same Protestant society was organized the Calvinistic spirit manifested as Puritanism. By an accident of war, the man who became most prominent in that connection was Oliver Cromwell.

---

*The origin of the so-called "Oxford Movement" did *not* spring from Newman and his group, but began much earlier, when a sermon in defence of the Sacrament of Penance was preached in the University Church of St. Mary the Virgin under the inspiration of the emigrant French priests of 1793. Procure (if possible) and read the booklet "Priestly Absolution at Oxford".

OLIVER CROMWELL

WE HAVE seen in the case of Laud one of the effects of the seventeenth-century struggle upon the Protestant side of that struggle. Laud was the type of leader of those English Protestants who tried to reconcile their departure from Catholic unity and some lurking sympathy with a memory of the Catholic past. In the same Protestant camp there was present an opposite, growing force of a much more active kind; what was soon called Puritanism. Of this force Oliver Cromwell is the representative type.

It is accident, of course, that has made him so; but for his emergence as a leader of genius during the English Civil Wars not he but almost any other one of his more energetic contemporaries on the same side might appear to us to-day the type of militant Protestant. But though it is an accident which made of Oliver Cromwell a symbolic figure, it is worth while examining his nature and fortunes in that capacity.

We have seen how the character of Protestantism as it grew, took on substance and developed a particular spirit, summed up in the name of Jean Calvin.* It is *his* main doctrines, *his* attitude towards the universe which has given tone and colour to the whole Protestant movement; and though men are affected by the Calvinistic spirit in many various degrees, from those who feel it vividly and profoundly to those who only feel it vaguely and superficially, wherever the Protestant type of mind exists it is Calvin at work.

We have also seen what the special marks of Calvin's doctrine were. He had accepted from earlier men the doctrine of salvation by faith alone; the idea that good works are of themselves of no profit to salvation. But though he was not the first to maintain this (for that matter there have

---

*Jean Cauvin, or Calvin (in Latin Calvinus—"The bald one"), was the son of the steward to the See of Noyar north of Paris. His father was excommunicated for peculation. He was dispossessed and warmly took up the anti-Catholic Cause. He is, of course, known in English as "John Calvin".

been many among the theologians who had, long before the Reformation, come perilously near to such an affirmation), it was he who affirmed it most firmly and with the clearest definition, and he who made it triumph. Equal in importance is Calvin's second point, summed up in the word "predestination." Not only does the Creator know who will be saved and who will be damned, not only must he have known it from all eternity, but also he must have willed it. Calvin admitted only one will in the universe; and by that will, not by man's own will, still less by man's own acts, was he saved or damned.

The third essential in the Calvinist spirit is the doctrine of "conversion." The individual knows by a personal revelation, vouchsafed to him privately at a particular moment, that he is one of God's elect, predestined to glory and beatitude, while around them are the great mass of those whom God has condemned to eternal misery.

To all this add Calvin's doctrine of church government. Calvin being a Frenchman, and therefore alive with the power and desire to organize a complete system, determined to erect against the universal Catholic Church a new church which should be the guardian of these new truths whereof he was the prophet. That church of Calvin's we know now to-day as the Presbyterian organization. It is important to remember that of those who came under the influence of the Calvinist spirit only a certain proportion, indeed a minority, adhered to its full scheme; many, including Cromwell himself, were sharply opposed to the idea of a strictly disciplined religious organization for the protection and propagation of a new religion. They argued that since private judgment was the essence of Protestantism, each congregation must be left free to believe and affirm what it chose; but the fact that there was this internal quarrel between the complete Calvinist Protestant and the more general Calvinist spirit of those who would not accept the organization of the Calvinist Church must not blind us to the essential Calvinism of the whole characteristically Protestant movement. Cromwell himself was an excellent example of this. He actually disliked the idea of a strict Presbyterian Church; he fought it not only with arguments but with armies. His own particular group called themselves "Independents," in order to emphasize their attitude. They would have nothing to do with what the Scotch call "The Kirk"; they proved this when it was attempted to impose Presbyterianism on England after the Scotch alliance which the English Revolutionary Party had formed in order to fight the King.

Yet, although he thus opposed the "Kirk," no one was more thorough-going in his Calvinist philosophy than Cromwell, no one went through a more violent personal "conversion," no one was more eager to assert "the indefectibility of the saints," that is, the Calvinist doctrine that those who had once felt "conversion" were ever after secure of salvation and could not lose grace. No one was more permeated with that spirit of prostration before the omnipotence and majesty of God than was Cromwell, no one was filled with a more violent zeal against the reprobate, no one in action was more ruthless against the enemies of the new religion.

The way in which Cromwell was typical of the whole Calvinist business is nowhere better seen than in his attitude towards the old religion which this new religion had set out to kill—that is, his attitude towards Catholicism. Catholicism was for him the very spirit of evil, to destroy which from off the face of the earth seemed to him the highest of the duties lying to his hand insofar as he could fulfil it. He could fulfil it to a considerable degree in this one Province of Europe, the British Isles, when he had achieved despotic power. And his intense fanaticism on this point appears especially in his treatment of Ireland. For the rest and in general, Cromwell was the typical figure of what is called Puritanism.

Puritanism is a particular form and degree of Protestantism which has specially flourished in England, Scotland and Wales, but of which there were wide areas throughout the Protestant world, notably in Scandinavia and in Holland. To be a Puritan is almost exactly the same as to be what the old world used to call a Manichaean. The Puritan and the Manichee have the same attitude towards the universe; their creeds work out to the same moral and social practice. But there is one doctrinal difference between them, for while the Manichee believes in an evil principle which works side by side with and is equal to the principle of good in the universe, the Puritan, proceeding from Calvin and therefore only admitting one will in the universe, makes both evil and good combine in the same awful God who permits, and in a sense wills, evil, and particularly the sufferings of man.

There is then this difference in doctrine between the two, the old heresy which continually reappears throughout the earlier Christian centuries and the new heresy of the sixteenth century. But in practice the effects of the two were just the same, and Puritanism made of the society which it affected very much what the Albigenses made of their society in the twelfth and thirteenth centuries and the Bulgarian heretics made of theirs in an earlier time still.

The sentiment rather than the conviction that the material world is evil, and therefore that all sensual joy is in essence evil, lies at the root of Puritanism. Joy in the arts, delight in beauty, and the rest of it, are the Puritan's object of hatred. He sees them all as rivals to the majesty of God and obstacles which deflect the pure worship of that majesty.

It has been remarked as a curious by-product of Puritanism that it threw men back on to the pursuit of wealth as their main occupation. It is from Puritanism that we derive modern industrial capitalism, the centralization of wealth in a few hands, the dispossession of the masses and their exploitation by a small number of those who control the means of production; all that we call Capitalism. But though industrial capitalism and its evils are a product of Puritanism, they are only so at second-hand. The Puritan of Oliver Cromwell's day, and Oliver Cromwell himself, the typical Puritan, was greedy of wealth indeed, but not as a single occupation of the mind, nor even as the chief business of man. The ardent occupation of Cromwell and those like him was the contemplation and worship of Calvin's sanguinary God; the defence of his proclaimed worship; and the extirpation of his enemies.

The accidents by which Oliver Cromwell became the typical figure of English Protestantism in its extreme or Puritanical form were these:

He was a cadet of one of those millionaire families who had gained their enormous wealth out of the wreck of the monasteries during the period of the Reformation. His father, of whom he was the only surviving son, was himself the only son of the enormously wealthy Sir Henry Cromwell, and Henry was the son of Richard Cromwell, nephew of Thomas Cromwell, the man who dissolved the monasteries under Henry VIII. Richard Cromwell's real name was Richard Williams. He was nephew to Thomas because his mother had been Thomas Cromwell's sister, his mother having married a tavern-keeper in Putney, near London, whose name was Williams. Richard took on his important relative's name, but both he and those who succeeded him had to use the name Williams for legal purposes, and when his great-grandson, Oliver, lay in state, the title "Oliver Cromwell, *alias Williams*," was embroidered on the half-royal hangings which draped the bed.

When his father died, Oliver Williams, alias Cromwell, inherited an income of what we should call to-day something rather more than £3,000 a year. But though his fortune was moderate, compared with many of his rank, what marked him out was the immense fortune of those to whom he belonged. The Reformation has been called "a rising of the rich against the poor." This does not apply to it in the remote valleys of Switzerland and the Scandinavian fells, but it is an epigram more than half true of its progress in England, and the fact that Oliver belonged to one of those millionaire families recently founded on the loot of religious endowments is highly characteristic of the whole time. The House of Commons to which he was returned as a young man was composed almost entirely of rich people like himself—great land-owners and their relatives, with here and there a prominent lawyer, or, quite exceptionally, a prominent merchant.

The English House of Commons was in those days a body only called together as a rule for brief periods. It was always summoned on the accession of a monarch, and whenever there was important and solemn law-making to be done it was summoned to confirm the King's will and to subscribe to what he and his Council and the great lords had decided. The Crown had become so poor in Cromwell's time that government could not be carried on without special voluntary grants by the owners of property, and for making these grants there was no one but the House of Commons. It took advantage of its position to attack the powers of the King and the quarrel ultimately ended in a civil war. Of the Parliament, the Lords for the most part hesitated to rise in armed rebellion; of their relatives and fellow landowners, the Commons, rather more than half or about half, were prepared to levy a regular war against the King. But even those of the richer classes who were reluctant to attack the Crown physically, were nearly all at heart opposed to the old claims of the Crown in government and they nearly all wanted at heart to supplant government by a king whose duty and function it was to protect the poor against the rich, the weak against the strong. They desired to supplant him and take over the government themselves. That in effect is what they did. They won their war, they put the King to death, and among them was the amateur soldier who so rapidly became the best professional soldier of his time: Cromwell.

He had a genius for forming and leading cavalry. No one suspected it, least of all himself, until the opportunity came which made it manifest. Cromwell was already in his forty-third year when the War broke out. He had barely entered his forty-fifth when it was clear he would become the principal military figure. He was installed the head of the victorious army by the time that he was forty-eight, and in his fiftieth year it was he who plotted for and achieved the death of King Charles. He proceeded to the conquest of Ireland, a task which he accomplished with horrible cruelty and as a result of which he dispossessed nineteen-twentieths of the Irish nation, confiscating their land wholesale. He intended to destroy the Catholic Church altogether in that country. He thought that he had achieved that end before he died; but there he was mistaken.

The Scottish Presbyterians had fought as allies of the Parliamentary Rebels during the Civil War, but the Scotch people had a strong feeling in favour of the Stuart dynasty which was itself Scotch in origin. They sent an army to save the King after he had lost the war in England, which army Cromwell defeated in the most brilliant of his campaigns. They tried to make the dead King's son take the place of his father and this gave Cromwell the opportunity for conquering Scotland as he had conquered Ireland. He died the complete master through his military machine of the three kingdoms and the possessor for the moment of the strongest military force in Europe.

All that political experiment of an English military republic under a "Protector" was ephemeral. It was bound to break down and did so within two years of Cromwell's death. He died on the third of September, 1658, and the dead King's son, young Charles, returned and was crowned Charles II in the Spring of 1660. Nevertheless, that for which Cromwell stood had, in effect, conquered.

Those who retained Catholic principles and inclinations in England were still very numerous; when he died they were still more than a quarter of the population. In Ireland, in spite of massacre and wholesale robbery the great Catholic mass stood firm, and there at least seven-eighths of the people retained their religion in spite of the conquest; but the Civil War had completed both in Britain and in Ireland that long process of Catholic impoverishment and Protestant enrichment which had begun with the Dissolution of the Monasteries more than a hundred years before and had been continued with the Irish confiscations under Elizabeth and completed with the enormous fines levied upon all those landowners in England who stood out boldly and openly proclaimed themselves Catholic.

Further, the victory of those for whom Cromwell stood and of whom he was the most conspicuous leader was the virtual end of the monarchy, although kingship had come back amid universal rejoicing before young Charles had been crowned at Westminster and all the rest of it. The great landowners and the great merchants, acting through the House of Commons and the House of Lords, which they formed, took over the government in England and have retained it ever since. Further, after that episode there could be no question of the Catholic Faith returning in any strength. It might have survived in a large fraction of the people, but it could never again mould the general spirit of England.

Oliver Cromwell, therefore, is not only the chief Puritan figure at the decisive moment, the seventeenth century, when the Protestant and Catholic separated finally and agreed to call it a drawn battle; he is also the figure who marks the turning point in the transformation of England from a Catholic to a Protestant country.

The process was not completed under him. Catholicism largely survived in England till it received its death blow there in 1688. But by the time of his death the Protestant character of England as a whole was firmly fixed.

RENE DESCARTES

IN THE midst of these political figures, Kings and Statesmen and Soldiers, whom we have been considering in connection with the great religious struggle of the seventeenth century, we must turn for a moment to two men who had no political power. They were neither Soldiers nor Statesmen nor men of any hereditary position; but they influenced the mind of Europe so greatly that their indirect effect weighed more than the direct effect of others.

These two men stood to each other in time as might a father to a son. Descartes, nearly the contemporary of Cromwell, was born in 1596 and died in 1650. Pascal was twenty-seven years younger, but died only twelve years after Descartes in 1662. It is remarkable to note how both of them survived to see the settlement in the political and military fields of the great quarrel between the Reformation and the Catholic Church.

On the political field that quarrel was settled, as we have seen, in 1648–49. The Peace of Westphalia (as the two treaties ending the Thirty Years' War are called) was very nearly contemporary with the execution of Charles I, the end of Richelieu's great work and all the rest of it. In other words, both Pascal and Descartes lived during and past the turning point; and the impress which each of them stamped upon European thought was given just before it was too late—that is, while the society of Christendom was still sufficiently warm from the struggle to take an imprint, but no longer in the boiling effervescence of the original conflict. Born a generation earlier Descartes and Pascal might have been heresiarchs: born a generation later the one might have been a mere eighteenth-century sceptic and the other a mere private devotee. As it was, their lives and activities were expended at a moment when they would be of maximum effect—challenging criticism without actual condemnation, and influencing the Catholic culture without at first any disruptive effect.

These two men represent the effects upon the Catholic culture of two very great forces let loose by the Reformation, or at any rate let loose by the

break-up of the old united Christian order in Europe. The first was Rationalism: the second may be called (I think with propriety) Emotionalism.
Both men remained orthodox throughout their lives, each could claim that
he was not only orthodox but strongly attached to the Catholic Church
and all that the Catholic Church believes and teaches, yet from them proceeded results which stretched throughout the Catholic culture and shook
its stability, while at the same time spreading far outside the boundaries of
the culture into the Protestant culture and affecting the whole of European
thought.

Of the two it was Descartes who did the most. He was undoubtedly the
greater man—indeed, intellectually one of the greatest men Europe has
ever produced. But negatively Pascal was also of high effect, because his
example and the power of his word fostered that non-rational dependence
upon emotion which is ultimately as disruptive of Catholic solidity as is
Rationalism.

Descartes was the man who started all that mode of thought which at
last, in the nineteenth century, became universal, and is only now beginning to be questioned; the mode of thought which we sum up under the
term "scientific", which refuses to accept an affirmation that cannot be
clearly stated and as clearly apprehended by the receiver, and refuses also to
accept any affirmation (however clearly stated or clearly apprehended) unless it is accompanied by absolute proof based on deduction or experience.
From Descartes there followed (as will I think be universally admitted) that
tendency in all philosophy called "modern" which till lately grew more and
more sceptical of mystery, less and less concerned with the unseen, and
more and more occupied with matters susceptible of repeated experiment
and physical appreciation. When a man talks of the doctrine of immortality, for instance, as "a speculation," while calling the chemical constitution
of water out of oxygen and hydrogen a fact, he is at the end of a process
which was begun by Descartes. Not that Descartes would have put anything so crudely and falsely as that, but from him proceeds the habit of
founding certitude upon either mathematical truth or physical experiment
or the two combined—and nothing else.

For instance, in that matter of the immortality of the soul: the man
who says he will not accept the immortality of the soul because there is
no "proof" of it, means that he requires either a mathematical deductive
proof proceeding from first principles which nobody doubts or can doubt,
or that he requires physical proof by experiment. Well, the man who says,
"I have come to believe in the immortality of the soul, since I attended a

Spiritualist séance," is just as much a product of the Cartesian effect upon the world as a man who will not believe in immortality because it has not been proved to him. The man who only begins to believe in immortality because he thinks he has heard the voice of a dead person, or has had some other communication with him susceptible of physical test is, in the sense wherein we are using that word, strictly "rationalist."

And at this point it is important to define our terms, for "rationalist" and "rationalism" are terms that may be used in many varying senses. We mean by the Cartesian rationalism that habit of subjecting all examination of reality (that is, all the search after truth) to a certain process which is called "that of the reason" and "the reason only." It is in reality far too narrow a definition of the word "reason," but it is that which the great bulk of men still give and still act upon. It is "reasonable" to accept the evidence of your senses; it is "reasonable" to accept a mathematical proof. But (they say) it is not "reasonable" to accept any truth on any other basis.

In contrast to this profound effect of Descartes, we mark the effect of Pascal under what has been termed "emotionalism." There is nothing out of the way tending to unorthodoxy, inimical to Catholic solidity, in reliance upon emotion. Where Pascal's influence may be called destructive, or at any rate weakening to the strength of the Catholic culture, is in the tendency to substitute emotion for reason; to take emotion out of its proper sphere and give it authority in places where it has none. Thus, we may say that Pascal (without in the least intending it) stood at the beginning of that recent movement called "Modernism"; and there has been an influence flowing from Pascal, an influence which he himself would have bitterly regretted had he seen its fruits, tending to ignore definition in morals and doctrine because definition is not an emotional process. There has also come from the same source a parallel tendency to deny any doctrine which shocks some emotion. Or again, to affirm as certain something which the Church has not defined but which suits the private emotion of the believer.

When we use the term "emotionalism" in this particular sense, just as when we use the word "rationalism" in its particular sense, we mean allowing emotionalism in the one case, as reason in the other, to do something it was not intended to do: to step outside its proper sphere. Here is an example of emotionalism at war with reason:

A modernist suffering from the ambient agnostic atmosphere of his time denies what he calls the "historical" Resurrection of Our Lord. Yet he insists on the spiritual value (or spiritual *truth* as he will even call it) of the Resurrection. He ends by the absurdity that there are two truths; one the truth that a thing actually happened, and the other the truth that whether it happened or not does not count so long as it creates a pleasing emotion, to which he falsely attaches the word "truth." Perhaps the most famous sentence of all that Pascal wrote is also the shortest example of this kind of thing. That sentence runs as follows: "The heart has its reasons of which the head knows nothing." This is perilously near to saying that emotion is certain of things which reason contradicts.

Both men were great mathematicians. Descartes much the greater. Both men were remarkable writers, Pascal much the greater. From Pascal you may say comes the whole habit of clear modern prose writing; and from Descartes comes the whole business of analytical geometry and the theory of the calculi, differential and integral.

The process whereby each of these men attained the position he did was very different in either case. Descartes approached the problem of the discovery of truth by a process of elimination. "What are we? Whence do we come? Whither do we go? What is the Universe and what are we therein?" To answer these prime questions he began by throwing overboard everything which he felt he could not, in the new scientific temper of the time, affirm. And he reached the residuum that the only thing of which he was absolutely certain—the only thing which he could take as a first postulate, the only thing "known" whence he could proceed to discover the unknown, was his own existence.

That postulate was undoubtedly true, but it was the postulate of a scep-tic, and it has acted ever since as a poison. For there is another thing of which we are also just as certain, really, as we are of our own existence—and that is the existence of things outside ourselves. There is no rational process by which the reality of the external universe can be discovered; all we know is that it can be confidently affirmed. Aristotle, who might be called reason itself; St. Thomas, whose whole process was that of beginning with a doubt, and examining all that there was to be said for that doubt before the denial of it and the corresponding certitude could be arrived at, both postulate this second truth. Not only am I, I, but that which is not myself is just as real as I am, and what is more, can be and is apprehended by myself.

That is, like all true philosophy, common sense. Your plain man, who is made in the image of God and who, so long as his reason and conscience are not warped, is on the right lines, has no patience with any denial of it. The whole of human society takes it for granted and must take it for granted. The witness in a Court of Justice, the man conducting his own affairs, the simplest activities of daily life, takes for granted as absolutely certain, not only the external universe in which we live, but our own power of apprehending it. Descartes returned to the very extreme of the old Greek scepticism, and said, "No, we must begin with the prime certitude of our own existence; from which, no doubt, we can proceed to a second certitude that the external world exists. But we must not take it as a primal postulate." Therefore, it is from Descartes that the whole stream of modern scepticism flows. He built up a system carefully and accurately from so exiguous a beginning; it was like building a pyramid upside down, balanced upon a point, yet that system was stable and indeed on all its main lines it has stood for 300 years. It included the idea which most men still have of space, of the universe in three dimensions and three dimensions only, of the value of physical experiment and the certitude of our scientific conclusions therefrom. Of the certitude also of our power of measurement, upon which all modern physical science is built. The philosophy of Descartes remained stable and held the field because it was supported and continued by the rising flood of physical science. In some of his detailed conclusions he was fantastic, and would seem particularly fantastic in modern eyes; but his general spirit conquered the European mind and directed it right on into the memory of men now living. Indeed, no small part of our bewilderment, when we hear the doubts or questions of the latest physical science, is due to our being disturbed in what we thought to be our quite secure Cartesian philosophy; namely, that matter and spirit are quite distinct, and that all time and motion are referable to fixed standards—and so forth. But there is no denying Descartes' far-reaching influence.

BLAISE PASCAL

PASCAL STARTED from the very other end from Descartes of the mental process; not from a search for the last ultimate thing of which reason is certain, but from that which emotion most poignantly affirms. With Descartes it was, "I am sure of one thing—that I think." With Pascal it was, "I am sure of one thing—that I feel." Descartes began like a man pursuing a piece of research in history or chemistry; Pascal began like a man moved suddenly by a vision or a great love. The one would have told you that he had done nothing until he had begun to analyse—the other that he had not lived until he had been overwhelmed by a spiritual flood from within.

There were two occasions in Pascal's life in which he suffered or enjoyed that experience which is often called "conversion." Each confirmed the other, without either he would not have been what he was, and it was under the influence of intense personal feeling in the matter of religion that he began his famous quarrel with the Jesuits—which quarrel is, I am afraid, the main source of his reputation in the anti-Catholic world. For the attitude of the anti-Catholic world towards Pascal, and particularly the academic Protestant world, is something like this:—"The Jesuits are the quintessence of Catholicism. Pascal attacked the Jesuits. Therefore, although we are very sorry that he remained orthodox and was never excommunicated we feel that he was on our side."

Indeed, within Pascal's own lifetime there were a great many people not at all on the Jesuits' side, nor speaking in favour of the Jesuits, who accused Pascal of bringing the Protestant tone of mind and even the Calvinist tone of mind by a back door into the Catholic Church. They were later to say the same thing of Fénelon. The root cause of the violent conflict between those of whom Pascal was the spokesman and the Jesuits was the fact that the Jesuits had made it their business to reconquer Europe for the Church; they had made the relief and reinforcement of the Church—that is, the collective thing whereby the individual lives—their objective (to use a military term for an effort that was essentially military in tone). "*Etre*

Catholique, c'est tout," as was said to me once by a very holy Polish priest on his death-bed in Rome. He had never been a Jesuit nor had much to do with them. But that is the core of the Jesuit matter—"to be Catholic is all."

Now, for Pascal and those who thought with Pascal, and of whom he was the voice and the pen (though not the leader), the individual was everything. Of course, all these phrases and epigrams are mere shorthand: in a sense the individual is everything; it is the individual soul that is damned or saved and the Church is only there to help a man to save it. But if in emphasizing this you are led to belittle the majesty of the Church, the Divinity of its authority, and the enthusiastic acceptation of its organic character, you are doing a very ill service to the individual.

If the Jesuits in Pascal's time had only represented this one tendency out of many, the quarrel would not have become as famous as it was. The Jesuits had also, by their discipline, their sacrifice of self and their soldierly characteristics, acquired and retained great power—a power not only social but political. The reaction against that power within the Catholic Church is symbolized by the term "Jansenism."

Cornelius Jansen was a Dutch prelate, born in the generation before Pascal, who had become Bishop of Ypres. He was the author of a big book, the brief title of which was the *Augustinus*. He drew, from a one-sided reading of St. Augustine, as have so many before and since, doctrines approaching and sometimes going across the borderline of heresy especially in the matter of free will. From him came the whole body of opinion called in France "Jansenism," the resemblance of which to Calvinism on account of this central tendency (which might almost be called an affirmation against the freedom of the will and the corresponding insistence upon Predestination) brought it into violent conflict with the Jesuits, whom the Jansenists accused of laxity. They said that the Jesuits, in their effort to reconquer Europe for Catholicism, had made things too easy for the world and its weaknesses. Especially did they attack those who among the Jesuits had favoured the more liberal and indulgent casuistical decisions.

The word "Casuist" has been very stupidly given a bad name by people who do not understand it. It simply means the application of morals to a particular case, and especially to a difficult case. For instance, the commandment of God forbids us to kill our fellowmen. But are there cases in which, in spite of this commandment, we may kill our fellowmen without sin? Ninety-nine people out of a hundred—indeed one might say almost all sane men—would answer, "Yes; in self-defence, in a just war, as a wise punishment, and perhaps in certain other cases." It is worth noting, by the way, that the most sentimental people, who are loudest against the right to wage a just war, or execute a criminal, are just the people who are most likely to be in favour of "putting incurables out of their pain," which the commandment against murder most emphatically forbids.

Anyhow, the laxer casuist writers among the Society of Jesus were made the special target of the Jansenist movement, when that movement had the good luck to secure the literary talent of Pascal on its side. Pascal launched out against the Jesuits and the more liberal, more humane, casuists in a series of famous pamphlets known as the *Provinciales*.

Their wit, their clarity, their gusto, made them immediately famous, and of intense effect upon the educated world of their time. As style they are beyond praise, they launched modern French prose and one may fairly say modern prose as a whole. But if that be true of their literary or aesthetic side, it is most emphatically not true of their intellectual side. Pascal had not read the casuists whom he attacked, he often misunderstood what they had said, he was often plainly ignorant even of their most obvious meaning because he had not read them, and he was downright wrong in the greater part of his conclusions. His attacks on Escobar make amusing reading, but it is false reading—he caricatures and he caricatures in ignorance. Chateaubriand was quite right when he said that Pascal in the *Provinciales* had achieved "an immortal lie." (*Pascal said he had read Escobar three times. He plainly had read him not once.*)

It is strange that the literary and spiritual influence of Pascal should repose as it does upon such a very small body of matter. Apart from the *Provinciales* the only thing of his that really counts is a jumble of disjointed aphorisms which have had to be edited and re-edited to give them any cohesion, which even so have no unity, and to which the title is generally given of the *Pensées* or "Thoughts" of Pascal. Two of his ideas at least were profound and of high value, quite apart from the merely aesthetic value of his power of the "Word." One of these was the somewhat whimsical but arresting conception of the "wager." It is not a rational conception, but it is calculated to make the sceptic think. It amounts virtually to this:—

If the Christian revelation be not true, I lose nothing by accepting it. If it be true, I gain everything by accepting it. As against this, I for my part will at once advance a certain sentence of St. Paul's, to the effect that if we are wrong in our choice, of the Christian revelation, then we are "of all men the most miserable."

The other and more valuable and what will, I think, prove the most permanent literary "find" of Pascal's was his famous paradox on the coincident greatness and littleness of man. He did not invent that idea of course; it is as old as human thought upon these things: Man is miserably weak, even physically; he is mortal, limited in all his powers, even those of the reason; subject to all manner of suffering and apparently unable to help himself, even where the path to a tolerable existence lies clear. But at the same time man is gifted with a mind which can conceive the universe, he is the child of God and in the image of God, all beauty is at his command, he can even in a sense create, he is vastly greater than anything else there is within our immediate experience, yet he is immeasurably less than what he knows he might be. He is at once despicable and awful; petty and supreme. That consideration on the contrasting and dual nature of man is perhaps the most fecund germ that can be planted in the soil of the mind—and Pascal planted it more surely and deeply than any other man in his brief statement.

But Descartes will outlast Pascal. The peril to Catholicism proceeding from the rationalism of Descartes was apparently greater than the peril proceeding from the emotionalism of Pascal—the one was like a storm let loose against the old and firmly rooted oak, the other was like a sudden narrower flood, a torrent of water attacking its base. The tempest was the greater, and, of the two forces, the more enduring in its results.

Or one might put it in this way:—

The exaggeration of personal emotion in religion cannot produce a mood whereby the man who has left Catholicism will return to it: but an exaggeration of the function of reason is an error on the right side, and those who follow that path are more likely to promote the return of the world to the Faith.

For Pascal the appreciation of any truth, especially a moral or religious truth, concerns the emotions. Faith in the mere formulae of doctrine would be a dead faith. In Emotionalism the action of the conscience is not that of a deductive rational process or even that of an experiment or of an appreciation of an object from without. It is an internal imperative order, which does not base itself upon a thought-out process or a deliberately sought experience, but on the immediate sense; it is an emotion, and nothing but an emotion, of right and wrong. The natural reaction of a healthy mind against, say, the betrayal of a friend, does not work by presenting to the mind a process of thought, by detailing the consequences of the act or analysing its character; the feeling is immediate and instinctive and we know in some fashion that we are bound to obey. We know that if we do not obey we are doing "wrong," and no analysis will carry us beyond that.

The thing is a postulate. One can see the consequences of such an over-emphasis on emotions.

However these things may be, these two great men stand for the reaction upon Catholicism as a whole produced by the upheaval of the sixteenth century and early seventeenth century—all that confused movement which has been called the twin warring brothers, Reformation and Renaissance. And when we consider all the effect of them, the way in which Descartes has led to sceptical rationalism, Pascal to a contempt for doctrine and a sort of cloud over the mind in which men lost the Faith, the most remarkable thing still is that both men remained firmly of the Faith, lived in it and died in it. They both were living proofs that the Gates of Hell had not prevailed and that the Church had proved its power to survive.

For my own part the two things that stand out most vividly in the case of either man are these:

Of Descartes, that he had the humility, the faith and the devotion to make the pilgrimage to Loretto; of Pascal, the splendour of his death.

WILLIAM OF ORANGE

WILLIAM OF ORANGE is the last but one of the typical figures of the great seventeenth-century "Drawn Battle" between advancing Protestantism and Catholic resistance. There were many Williams in this family, and more than one have the title of Orange. But when one talks of "William of Orange" without additional words, one generally means this particular William of Orange, who became, so far as the rich men of England could make him so, the King of England at the end of the seventeenth century. On the Protestant side of the battle he corresponds to—though a man of far less importance—the Catholic Louis XIV. He stands for the successful Protestant resistance which caused the battle to be a drawn one; just as Louis XIV, his contemporary, stands for the later declining, but still most powerful, Catholic tradition in the west of Europe.

Of how far Louis XIV fills this role, and how the very fact that he does not fill it altogether but only in a mixed way is characteristic of the time, I shall describe in my next chapter.

William of Orange, the antagonist of Louis, is then typical of the Protestant side of the "Drawn Battle" in every way.

To begin with, he is typical of the way in which the great leaders, who made the survival of Protestantism possible and secured its further expansion, were not—as had been the early zealots of the Reformation—men chiefly occupied with religion. They were men chiefly occupied with political power, and to an almost equal, sometimes to a greater extent, with the great personal income to be derived from political power. They were not men chiefly marked for their enthusiasm against the Catholic creed and practice, but rather marked for their determination to establish their independence from the old unity of Europe, and men who depended for their power upon wealth.

The way in which William III came into the great quarrel was as follows: The family, of which he was the head, was the ancient family of the Counts of Nassau; Nassau being the name of a town and of a medieval government, district or county, in the western part of Germany, near Wiesbaden.

These Counts of Nassau had been the officials governing the district, and their power had become hereditary and feudal not long after Charlemagne. William, therefore, was the representative of a family something like a thousand years old. He counted among the very ancient and high nobility of western Europe. This family of Nassau had married one of their women to the feudal Chief of the town and district of Orange, on the Rhone, near Avignon, just at the time when the Reformation was beginning to stir, that is, shortly after 1500. The last Prince of Orange in the regular line died childless in the years when Henry VIII of England was agitating for his divorce, and when the Reformation in Germany was beginning to strike deep roots. He left his Lordship of Orange by will to his nephew of Nassau, and thence onwards the family of Nassau, or rather the successive heads of the family, were called "Princes of Orange."

As yet they were only important, ancient and fairly wealthy nobles of that old feudal sort who were becoming (with the Renaissance) modern local rulers. But one of them who came immediately after (generally called "William the Silent") happened to fall heir to several very large fortunes which all concentrated upon himself. As quite a young man he was already one of the richest men in Europe, and had a corresponding power in the politics of the day. This William, Count of Nassau, was born a little before Henry VIII married Anne Boleyn; and died, assassinated, a little before the failure of the Spanish Armada expedition against England. He was, roughly speaking, a contemporary of Queen Elizabeth, but a few years older. This elder William of Nassau, Prince of Orange, has obtained in history the name of "William the Silent" in rather an absurd fashion, and he certainly has no right to it.

Let us see how that name arose. As a very young man, or rather boy, he had been a sort of hostage at the French court to insure the carrying out of a treaty between the King of France and the Emperor Charles V. Many years afterwards when he had abandoned the Catholic religion and was in full rebellion against his legitimate sovereign, he brought out a cock-and-bull story to the effect that during his youth at the French Court the King had confided to him a plot for massacring all Protestants. He himself, William, boasted that on hearing this terrible news he had been horrified, but had cunningly kept silent; and he gave it to be understood that it required no small courage and intelligence for a youth of his years to have acted so discreetly under the circumstances.

The story William thus told long after in later life is an obvious falsehood. He said not a word about it between the supposed time of its taking place and the moment when, according to his account, he chose to "release it." That a powerful King would have confided such a vital State secret to a lad is even less credible than the story of the plot itself, or the likelihood of the boy and the man remaining completely silent about it for half a lifetime, during years when the news would have been of vital importance. However, the times were fanatical. Almost anything was believed by one side against the other. William was astute and he got away with it. The Protestant side of Europe affected to believe the story, which you will now see solemnly repeated in most of our textbooks; and that comic nickname "the Silent" remains attached to William, and will presumably always so remain.

This William "the Silent", being the wealthiest and the most important subject in the Netherlands, was tempted to take the lead in rebellion against the lawful Government of those countries.

The lawful Government was that of Philip II of Spain. There was nothing unnatural or odd about the King of Spain being thus also monarch of a district which is to-day divided into Holland and Belgium. Political power over widely separated European districts went in those days everywhere by legitimate descent; and Philip of Spain was the inheritor, through the woman of the Burgundian house, of those who had been the lawful monarchs ruling the seventeen provinces of the Netherlands. These provinces and their great mercantile cities had prospered under the house of Burgundy, to which they were much attached, and, after that house had ended in a heiress, it seemed to them quite natural and right that her grandson, Philip, should be their monarch.

But there were two troubles ahead. The first, much the most important, was the outbreak of the great religious rebellion against Catholicism, which led to rioting and fighting between Reformers and Orthodox all over the west of Europe. The second was the fact that the great kingships of the day were tending to become absolute and to neglect local liberties.

Now the great trading towns of the Netherlands, which were the maritime emporiums for the vast traffic of the Rhine, the Meuse, and the Scheldt (Ghent, Antwerp, Brussels, Lille, Arras, Bruges, etc.), had, like all mercantile communities of the later Middle Ages, enjoyed a large measure of local self-government. They were jealous of any encroachment upon this. When the Religious Revolution broke out (with its violent local riots and disturbances, endless fights of Reformers against Orthodox), the fact that the King of Spain stood for the old orthodox tradition made it natural that those who feared for their local political liberties should in many cases flirt with the new revolutionary ideas in religion, and this they did. In other words a considerable number of the principal merchants and rich men in the towns of the Netherlands took up Calvinism; and this new religion was also avowedly the religion of those who had broken out in the riots and looting of Church property, including the accompaniments of murder and torture. (The tortures which the revolutionaries had inflicted upon the monks were particularly horrible.)

The regular Government of Philip II set out to suppress these disorders, but it needed money for the task. The money which had been sent for the paying of the troops was held up in the English ports on its way from Spain by the man who governed England in the name of Elizabeth, William Cecil. The Government of the Netherlands was therefore forced to levy a special tax to replace the money. This tax, in a commercial community like that of the Netherlands, was intensely unpopular, and armed revolt broke out all over the country. This was the opportunity for the rich men who wanted to make political capital out of the troubles and increase their income at the same time, and of these the richest naturally became the leader. Therefore the multi-millionaire William "the Silent" appeared as the chief name in the rebellion. For a long time he hesitated to abandon Catholicism. But it seemed upon the whole the card to play; for though the rebellion was not mainly religious but mainly political and economic, Calvinism was part of the driving power behind it. Philip II, King of Spain, to whom and to whose family William had owed everything, outlawed William "the Silent," and a Catholic zealot shot and killed him in the year 1584. It is characteristic of the times that this assassination took place in a convent which had been confiscated and robbed by William's family. You may see to this day the marks of the bullets against the wall by the door where he fell, in the town of Delft.

After that the family of Orange (Nassau) though not uninterruptedly head of the rebels in the Netherlands remained always the typical leaders. The second son of William "the Silent" was a great soldier in the struggle of the Calvinist merchants of the northern Netherlands against Spain, and when things settled down in the middle of the seventeenth century (more than sixty years after William "the Silent's" assassination), a younger son of his was the chief man in Holland, which had by this time become practically independent. The son of this chief man, whose name again was William, married the Princess Mary of England, sister of Charles II. He died in November, 1650, and just after his death his wife bore the son who was again christened William, the hereditary name of the family, and he became known in English history as "William III," William of Nassau, Prince of Orange and King of England.

The child born under such strange circumstances grew up of a mixed sort. He was not without energy, though it was of a morose and silent kind. He had a strong aquiline nose, piercing eyes, and his dwarfish body, suffering from poor health and later from asthma, was not without vigour, but he was sullen and vicious. He was in general detested by those who came closest in contact with him, except the favourites whom he loaded with gifts and who were in some unknown degree partners in his vices. The first of these was a certain Bentinck, a man of good family. Later in life William very disgracefully took up with a too beautiful boy of unknown origin, called Keppel. When it came to marriage he had the good fortune to get for a wife his first cousin, Mary Stuart, grandchild, like himself, to Charles I of England, and daughter of James, Duke of York, who was later to be James II of England. The marriage was intrigued for, perhaps reluctantly, but at any rate decisively, by Charles II, who was King of England at the time, and who wanted to keep a foot in both camps, Catholic and Protestant. There were no children of that marriage, and the Princess Mary was next door to being deficient, so unintelligent was she. But the extreme importance of the marriage lay in this: that the wife this young William of Orange had married was the next heir to the throne of England at the time when her father, James II, should succeed his brother, Charles II.

This Mary, William's wife, had been brought up a Protestant, as a piece of state-craft insisted upon by Charles II, her uncle, who was the reigning king during her girlhood. He hoped thus to save the dynasty by counteracting the effect of his brother's conversion. Mary's mother, Anne Hyde, the daughter of Lord Clarendon, a woman of strong character and intelligence, had been converted to Catholicism, and she had brought over her husband, James, Duke of York, Mary's father, who was the immediate heir to Charles II. By the time James became King, Anne Hyde was dead. There was no boy to inherit the kingdom after James II died. James II's second wife, Mary of Modena, was of bad health and had lost her children. It was believed she would have no more. When this Catholic king came to rule, it was over an England which was by this time Protestant as to the great majority of its inhabitants, and as to a large minority of those inhabitants violently anti-Catholic (especially in London). Yet even those who most disliked the idea of the Catholic James being king over the country, and who had intrigued against his succession, were half prepared to accept him—because they took it for granted that he would be succeeded by his Protestant daughter Mary, the Princess of Orange. Not only was she a Protestant, but she was married to the man who was regarded as one of the leaders of the Protestant cause on the Continent of Europe.

It was in 1685 that James II had become English King. The discontent of the active Protestant minority led to rebellions in Scotland and in the South. They were easily put down. That in the South had been led by an illegitimate son of the late King, Charles II. This illegitimate son was called the Duke of Monmouth. He had no particular religion, but he took up the Protestant cause with violence, and naturally enough, as it was his best chance of getting rid of his uncle, James II, and of capturing the throne for himself. He gave it out that Charles II had married his mother. A very large number of the more intense anti-Catholics in the country believed this legend, and a still larger number were prepared to let it pass for truth so that they might have a Protestant champion immediately at hand against the reigning Catholic King. But when Monmouth's rebellion had been put down, and Monmouth himself executed, there remained, even for those who believed that Monmouth had been legitimate, no leader of the Protestant cause, no one whom they could regard as a possible substitute for James II, except his daughter Mary, and her husband, James' son-in-law, William of Orange.

The whole thing was mixed up with the now determined policy of the rich English families to take over the government of the country, and in their own selfish interests to destroy what was left of power in the crown. There was not much left of such power. The crown had become the puppet of the wealthy landed classes in England, who assumed the government of the country unchecked, through their two great committees, the House of Commons and the House of Lords, which were composed of their own landed class. They would far rather have had a new King, who should owe his nominal title to them, than to have the legitimate King James, who had behind him the full traditions of monarchy. But to these traditions, the masses of the English people were still strongly attached, and the wealthier classes who desired to get rid of the King and to take over the Government for their own advantage, could not openly upset the principle of monarchy in the face of popular opposition. It would be their object, I repeat, to have someone *called* king who should replace James II, but they would take care that this new king should have no real power and should be their servant.

So things stood until, in the fourth year after James' accession, a son was born to him, and the child lived. That changed everything. A Catholic king, surrounded by many Catholic advisers and friends, one determined to preserve royal power, and insisting upon religious toleration (so that the Catholic minority, which was something from an eighth of the people upwards, should have offices of trust in spite of their religion), had now an heir who would be brought up a Catholic, and who ousted his Protestant half-sister Mary, Princess of Orange, hitherto the natural successor to her father.

But those who were determined to get rid of James were not disarmed by this misfortune which had befallen them. There followed a series of the worst plots, conspiracies, and falsehoods in English history. A perfect orgy of lying, cheating and betrayal. William of Orange sent over to England an illegitimate relative of his, who had married an English wife, giving him the special message to congratulate James on the birth of an heir, and at the same time to intrigue secretly with anyone he could get hold of for turning James out and the new-born child with him. William of Orange further began to intrigue in Holland for the support of the Dutch. He began to try to raise money from the Dutch bankers on the securities of the taxes which his backers would, if he were made king, impose on the English. While he was doing this he protested in the loudest manner his loyalty to his father-in-law, James, and continued to proclaim that loyalty until the very hour of sailing with a large expedition to invade James' Kingdom.

James had a considerable army with which to defend his throne, but the officers were drawn from the landed classes who were conspiring against the throne and were ready to betray their King. William's force landed in Devonshire. It was made up of mercenary soldiers drawn from every country, with only a few Englishmen among them. Most of the officers were French Protestants, rebels, but the strongest thing in the force was the finely disciplined and armed Dutch (Blue) Guards of William himself.

There was no battle, because just when the issue would have been joined James was betrayed. The leader of those who betrayed him was John Churchill, later Duke of Marlborough, whose career as a soldier James himself had made. The Prince of Orange marched on London. The Dutch Guards occupied the western part of that town and appeared before the Palace. James was thrown out, and the rich men who had helped William of Orange made him their king. After long negotiations, he and his wife were declared equal partners, King and Queen side by side; so that the reign of the usurper is now officially known as that of "William and Mary."

Politically the thing was a complete revolution, or coup d'état: that is, an illegal, unconstitutional act of force by which a legitimate Government is supplanted. The English hereditary monarchy was disposed of, and a new, unheard of title called "Parliamentary title" was substituted for right of birth. The legitimate King, James II, lived on in France, protected by the King of France, his cousin Louis XIV. He attempted to get back his throne with the help of the French King, both through an Irish land campaign and through a maritime one in the Channel. He failed in both enterprises, and died at the beginning of the next century, within a few months of the son-in-law who had betrayed and dethroned him, and some time after the unnatural daughter who had aided her husband to act in this manner. The claim of the legitimate Stuart line was not given up, but their Catholicism was a fatal bar to their restoration, and they died out within a century, their attempts to regain the throne all proving futile.

In this way the work of the Reformation in England was accomplished. What had been, when James II was betrayed, an active minority of the nation—about sixteen per cent of the whole—still in actual Catholic practice (and many more in varying degrees of sympathy with the old religion) dwindled to an insignificant handful. Within one long lifetime, by, say, 1760, the practising Catholics had fallen to be less than one per cent of the population. What was perhaps more important, the non-practising "penumbra" of sympathisers with Catholicism had disappeared.

The link with the old national tradition was broken for ever, and when the Catholic Church began to flourish again in England it flourished as a foreign thing inspired first by French, later by Irish emigrants.

In the great "Drawn Battle" of the seventeenth century, of which England had been one of the principal fields, the decision, so far as England was concerned, was complete. The Protestant cause had completely won, more completely by far than in any other country in Europe. With that victory the name of the perverted William of Orange, though he was but a servant and a tool throughout, will always be associated.

LOUIS XIV

LOUIS XIV, the great king of France whose reign covers the last half of the seventeenth century, is the typical figure on the Catholic side of the great "Drawn Battle." He is what we may call the "opposite number" to William of Orange, though ten times greater and more important. There was no one on the Protestant side as yet, standing out sufficiently to make a prominent figurehead for that side. Therefore William of Orange is always regarded (in the later part of his life at least, after about 1680) in that capacity. Later the typical figures opposed to Catholic France, and to the Catholic German Empire, were the kings of Prussia. In less than a lifetime after Louis XIV's death, Frederick the Great of Prussia became the champion of the increasingly powerful anti-Catholic cause in Europe. But as early as 1650–1700 it is the house of Orange, and, in the later part of the period, William III of England, who represents, as we have seen, the resistance of the Protestant minority in Christendom.

It is very important when we are following the history of all this, not to "read history backwards"; that is, not to think of Europe as she later became, a civilization divided into two more or less equal halves, the Catholic culture and the Protestant culture, with the latter gradually advancing and the former divided against itself. In the later seventeenth century at the end of the "Drawn Battle" the Protestant culture had saved itself but it was still very much weaker than the Catholic. It included the small populations of Scandinavia, the Dutch merchants of Holland and the majority of their dependents (for Holland had a very large Catholic minority), Great Britain, and a certain proportion—perhaps one-third—of the populations who spoke German. But the overwhelming majority of Europeans were still Catholic. The Greek Church had as yet no weight, for Russia had not yet risen to be a power affecting the affairs of Europe, and the Balkan States were under the government of the Turk.

On this account the men who led the Protestant culture everywhere regarded themselves as being on the defensive; they were maintaining what they felt to be a very difficult and gallant resistance against greatly superior forces, and the fact that they were able to make the battle a drawn one reinforced their courage and confidence in themselves.

Louis XIV, by far the most powerful government on the Catholic side, was typical of the mixed state into which the religious cause had fallen. He was typical also of the way in which what had been a fairly clean-cut issue in the first lifetime of the Reformation—the issue as to whether the Catholic Church should or should not survive, whether the new heretics should also not break up civilization—had gradually settled down to something more complicated, much mixed up with local and individual interests. It had become on the Protestant side not only a question of maintaining Protestant culture, but (for the leaders) of keeping the enormous fortunes which they had suddenly made out of looting the Church during the troubles. Meanwhile, on the Catholic side, the defence of the general civilization of Christendom and of its old traditions was confused and debased by something much less ideal, to wit, the particular national and dynastic ambitions of this and that Catholic monarch. That was why the French, during the whole affair, were hostile to the Empire; why Paris and Vienna, the two centres of Catholic civilization, were hostile to each other. And that is why you so often find Rome in alliance, or half-alliance, with non-Catholic forces against the private ambitions of the Catholic Prince.

Louis XIV's whole reign, from when he ascended the throne as a little boy to when he died as an old man in 1715, is illustrative of this. He was the head of the Catholic cause, the strongest individual power in that cause, and yet he devoted half his energy to keeping the French Church wholly subject to his Government and resisting Papal authority therein, and all his energy to reducing Catholic Austria.

What is called "Gallicanism," the idea of national churches existing within the unity of the Catholic Church and yet maintaining highly developed local powers, was the special creation of Louis XIV and his reign. Both at the height of his power at the end of the second third of the seventeenth century, and in the decline of it in the last twenty years of his life, the national and dynastic motive of Louis was at least as strong as the religious motive, and often stronger.

Apart from Louis XIV's championship of Catholicism was his armed excursion by invasion of his neighbours.

The true explanation of Louis XIV's continually carrying on war outside his own country is to be found in the immediate past of that country and of his predecessors upon the throne.

France had been, almost up to his birth, the battlefield of the two religions. Calvinism, the fighting force of the Reformation, and the spirit
which gave it all its driving power, was a French thing. The French nobility had taken it up as a weapon to use against the monarchy. There was a
moment when it looked as though France would have gone Protestant;
even as it was, although this revolution did not succeed, a furious civil war
raged for half a lifetime. Richelieu in the years before Louis XIV's birth had
saved the French monarchy from the aristocratic rebels, and prevented the
Protestant success, but at the expense of leaving the Protestants a strong
minority. Even after Richelieu's death, when Louis XIV was the boy king
of France, there had been a violent rebellion against the throne which had
driven the Court out of Paris.

With the French thus divided among themselves and indulging in their
favourite folly of civil war, they naturally and inevitably suffered invasion.
Time and again foreign armies came in from the Spanish Netherlands
(what to-day we call Belgium) and from the German Empire. All this tradition of peril and actual experience of it in childhood had so impressed
the mind of Louis that when he came to possess power—after he was eighteen—he was determined upon establishing two things: absolute unity and
peace within the realm and security beyond the frontiers.

"Either," he said, "I must suffer invasion, or I must establish myself in a
strong position beyond my frontiers."

When the King of Spain died Louis claimed, through his wife, a Spanish
Princess, the right to govern the Spanish Netherlands in her name. On his
attempt to enforce this right by arms followed all the fighting with which
his name is associated in what to-day is Belgium. The predominance of the
French power in Belgium alarmed the Calvinist Dutch merchant oligarchy
who governed what is to-day Holland, and who had only just established
their independence from Spain. They found they had got rid of the power
of Spain immediately to the south of them, in Brussels, only to see the
much more formidable power of France, with great armies, immediately
at their doors. The Dutch would sometimes ally themselves with Louis
XIV in order to lessen this danger; more often they would be openly his
enemies, but whether actually hostile or nominally allied, they always regarded Louis XIV as the great danger to their new state.

England, after the restoration of the legitimate king, Charles II, who was
Louis XIV's first cousin, could be used from time to time as an ally by Louis; but very uncertainly, for Charles II was determined to keep his throne
over a nation now predominantly Protestant and jealous of French power.

Charles II, therefore, skilfully played off the Dutch against Louis, and both of them against his own rebellious and disloyal wealthier classes, whose main effort was directed to lowering the power of the English crown. Elsewhere in Europe, the Empire, the Papacy, and the Spanish throne, were all intermittently, but generally, hostile to Louis' scheme of making his realm secure from invasion by establishing himself in power upon and beyond his frontiers. After the Stuarts had fallen, and James II had been turned out of England by the successive conspiracies of the wealthier classes, the Government of England joined in the general coalition against Louis XIV's old age, and William III, and after him the Duke of Marlborough during Queen Anne's reign, were leaders in battles which were fought with the one object of reducing the French power.

The attack on Louis XIV was sufficient to exhaust French wealth and man power, but it did not succeed in carrying on the invasion to the heart of France (it very nearly succeeded in this), nor did it succeed in shaking the power of the French dynasty, or breaking up the unity of the French nation.

The last piece of fighting at the very end of Louis XIV's reign turned upon the succession to the huge Spanish Empire at home and beyond the Atlantic. This had been left by will to the grandson of Louis XIV, and Louis XIV determined to maintain that grandson's claims. He succeeded in this. The Spanish Empire was governed by that younger branch of his family for a hundred years to come. In the struggle, the Spanish Netherlands, which Louis had claimed to govern, with their capital at Brussels, were taken out of the Spanish Empire and given to Austria, in whose hands they remained until the wars of the French Revolution.

Regarded therefore politically, Louis XIV's reign as a whole was the triumph of himself as a person, and of the French power. Though not the triumph of the Catholic cause in Europe which as we have seen was divided, at any rate his rule established the maintenance of preponderant Catholic power in Europe.

But France only achieved this position at the expense to Catholic culture of continually supporting the smaller Protestant powers in Germany against the Empire. Even in the English struggle Louis XIV was lukewarm. When the issue lay between the success or failure of James II in Catholic Ireland, Louis XIV, though willing to help his cousin, only consented to do so in a very half-hearted fashion, with few men—just enough to keep up the Catholic resistance in Ireland, but not enough to make that resistance finally successful.

If we turn from the political side to the purely religious, we find in Louis XIV's reign the source of nearly all that has followed on the Catholic side in Western Europe from that time onward, and particularly the source of what has happened in France.

The situation stood thus when Louis XIV had come to the throne as a boy: French Protestantism, led by many of the great nobles, backed by their wealth, and numerically strong all over the place, but especially in the south, was in a kind of hostile truce against the rest of the nation and of the Catholic monarchy which governed it. But socially things were going in favour of the old religion. As the young King increased in power, won victories beyond the frontiers and led his French civilization which morally dominated Western Europe, the greater and lesser Protestant nobles began to waver. Their religious feelings had never been so strong as their political, and indifference or conversion became commoner and commoner among them.

It is probable that if the pressure had been allowed to go on uninterruptedly it would have ended in the disappearance of most of the Huguenot centres, and France would have been as uniform in culture as England later became upon the other side. But at a critical moment about halfway through the reign, a grave error was committed. The King thought he could hasten the process of unity and proceeded to outlaw the Calvinist religion in his dominions. Men professing Calvinism could no longer hold office or officer's rank. Every obstacle was put in the way of the practice of the Calvinist religion, even in private, and a worse feature was the quartering of troops upon recalcitrant districts, especially in the central mountains where Protestantism had a hold upon the middle and lower middle classes, and even, in some places, upon the peasantry.

The sufferings and brutalities accompanying this policy have been exaggerated, as such things always are, but they were very great. A considerable number of the French Protestants who could afford to do so, emigrated. Those who remained behind, many of them very wealthy men holding a disproportionate number of posts in the commerce and finance of the country, were roused to a tradition of hatred against the monarchy, and of course to still stronger hatred of the traditional national religion. It was from this that, later on, the opposition to the principle of monarchy in France, and the fashionable anti-clericalism of the eighteenth century proceeded.

This sudden decision of Louis XIV to impose unity by force is known as "The Revocation of the Edict of Nantes," because, a lifetime before, it was by an edict called the "Edict of Nantes" that the French Protestants had been given their privileges, when the great religious wars had ended in a sort of truce.

It was with this "Revocation of the Edict of Nantes," as with so many other things in history. An apparent success proved, in the long run, not only to be a failure, but the weakening and threatened destruction of what had seemed to be the successful side.

There is a close parallel between all this and the corresponding action of England against Ireland, where the effort was also one to impose unity by force. There, an effort which at first apparently succeeded, to the complete ruin of the Irish people and their religion, was found after about a century—the same lapse of time as tested the French business—to have failed. It left behind a permanent source of weakness to the victor.

But if we sum up the reign of Louis XIV as a whole we see it in this light: it finally sets the seal on the European reaction towards Catholicism which had begun more than fifty years before Louis XIV was born. As to France herself, his Court, the great poets who lived in it or influenced it, the great prose writers, the great Churchmen, the great Generals—all made French influence, and therefore in a high degree the Catholic culture as a whole, the normal culture in Western Europe.

When Louis XIV died the 'Drawn Battle" appeared to have been settled once and for all on its last lines. The small but vigorous Protestant culture had been maintained, and was in possession of Great Britain, Scandinavia and a large minority of the German-speaking people; but the Catholic culture was still overwhelmingly the most numerous in Europe, and seemed secure from further molestation.

As is nearly always the case, the thing which seemed obvious to contemporaries was, as a fact, an illusion. Catholic culture in Europe was to meet a new foe within its own body, to wit, the sceptical anti-religious movement which has marked all the last two hundred years in France and Italy. The small Protestant powers were destined to increase vastly in political strength, and still more in wealth through commerce and activity overseas.

But all that was for the future. The death of Louis XIV may be taken to be the final term of the great see-saw struggle of the seventeenth century. The "Drawn Battle" had resulted by 1715 in the position I have described.